GOOD VIBES
365

Practical Prompts for Awareness, Writing, and Transformation

Laura Di Franco

Good Vibes 365: Practical Prompts for Awareness, Writing, and Transformation

Laura Di Franco

©Copyright 2022 Laura Di Franco

Published by Brave Healer Productions

Paperback ISBN: 978-1-954047-91-4

eBook ISBN: 978-1-954047-90-7

DEDICATION

*To anyone having trouble getting themselves
out of the pit of self-doubt, fear,
uncertainty, depression, or shame—
you can feel better.*

*You have the power to shift your energy and mood. You
were born, so you're worthy.*

You matter. The world needs you and your gifts.

Go for the joy. You were born for it.

Let's raise our vibes together.

DISCLAIMER

This book offers wellness information and is designed for educational purposes only. You should not rely on this information as a substitute for, nor does it replace professional medical advice, diagnosis, or treatment. If you have any concerns or questions about your health, you should always consult with a physician or other healthcare professional. Do not disregard, avoid, or delay obtaining medical or health-related advice from your healthcare professional because of something you may have read here. The use of any information provided in this book is solely at your own risk.

Developments in medical research may impact the health, fitness, and nutritional advice that appears here. No assurances can be given that the information contained in this book will always include the most relevant findings or developments with respect to the particular material.

These tools, practices, and knowledge have been shared with you with a sincere and generous intent to assist you on your health and wellness journey. Please contact me with any questions you have about the techniques or information provided.

TABLE OF CONTENTS

Introduction | i

PART ONE:

Good Vibes for the Body | 1

PART TWO:

Good Vibes for Your Mind | 102

PART THREE:

Good Vibes for Your Soul | 174

PART FOUR:

Shifting to Good Vibes
from Anger or Rage | 240

PART FIVE:

Other Kinds of Good Vibes | 264

In Conclusion | 371

With Huge Appreciation | 372

About the Author | 373

INTRODUCTION

The power to lift your mood, shift your energy, raise your vibration, feel better, and align with your deepest desires and dreams for the life you crave lies in your ability to recognize you have the choice to think, believe, and act differently. With awareness, you get that choice. That's badass!

There's amazing science behind the power of shifting your thoughts, energy, and vibration and how that works to retrain your brain and behaviors. I've been positively and forever influenced by folks like Esther Hicks, Joe Dispenza, John F. Barnes, Eckhart Tolle, and Byron Katie, and I have learned a thing or two about the practice of raising your vibration to manifest the life you crave.

Back in 2016, I went through a divorce. And while that event was my choice, I still experienced what I consider to be one of the worst years of my life. I'd been a pretty positive person all my life, and it felt like it took a Herculean effort to shift my vibe most days that year.

But I did. And I not only survived, my ex and I managed to move through that year without hiring lawyers or exposing our children to undue nastiness. I made good vibes and joy a priority as much as I could. It paid off, and I've experienced some pretty incredible moments since then. I made the practice of awareness and flipping my switch from negative to positive vibes my lifestyle and discipline. And I started to get better at it until it became the way I live, love, and be.

As life tends to happen, more tough days came my way several years later. These were experiences I found even more challenging. They tested my resilience and my practice. They made me bump up against my capacity to cope, mentally and emotionally. *I'm not sure I can do this*, I thought as I made my way into a courtroom to defend my daughter against her abuser.

And still, it was the same present-moment practice that saved me from relentless helplessness and anxiety and created a stronger version of me. Shifting from fear to love—mastering that—helped me become stronger, better, and more of everything I wanted to be.

VIBE SHIFTER

I wrote this book to give you more awareness and some easy tools to help you move from negative to positive vibrations (one for each day of the year); 365 ways to shift your vibe. It's a resource book you can pull out and use any time you feel bad, fall into the pit of self-doubt or fear, or anytime you feel yourself dwelling in negativity. This is a book of ideas, tools, techniques, and inspiration to shift your energy. Higher vibrations attract more high vibes. Who couldn't use a few more of those!?

WRITING PROMPTS

You can follow the pages in order or simply open up the book and read any good vibe to start! I encourage you to use the blank space for therapeutic journaling. I created this book with my writers in mind.

Writing is a powerful energy-shifting tool! Write down your thoughts, desires, worries, dreams, lists of to-dos—whatever needs to move from the inside of you to the outside. Or you can write about how the tool made you feel. My favorite journaling tool is the love list. Write about what you love, and your vibe shifts instantly.

For each vibe shifter, challenge yourself to use the sensation as a writing prompt. Grab your notebook and pen (or use the blank space on these pages), set a timer for three or five minutes, and write as fast as you can without censoring yourself. Write with the intention to Feng Shui your soul.

If any of the prompts are impossible to complete as described, visualize them. Your brain doesn't know the difference. Stay safe. Make it easy. Come up with your own versions of the activities and prompts. Have fun!

I hope you deeply enjoy reading and using this book as much as I enjoyed writing it for you!

Big love,

Laura

PART ONE

GOOD VIBES FOR THE BODY

When you use your body to shift your vibe, you have a powerful mind-clearing, soul-cleansing tool. Your body is the sacred vessel from which you experience everything. It's the portal to transformation. Here are some simple ways to raise your vibration using the power of your physical body.

1. Breathe

Stop for a moment to take ten slow, deep breaths, relaxing a little bit more with each exhale.

Use the space here to write about how that feels:

....

....

....

....

....

....

....

....

....

....

....

....

....

....

....

....

....

....

....

....

2. Stretch your neck

Sit down on a comfortable chair and slowly drop your head forward and to each side without feeling any pain, just a mild, comfortable stretch. Do this in super slow motion, giving yourself enough time to notice sensations at every degree of the angle. Remember to breathe.

Use the space here to write about how that feels:

....

....

....

....

....

....

....

....

....

....

....

....

....

....

....

....

....

....

3.   Giggle

Force a belly laugh. Start fake-giggling. Do that for ten seconds. See what happens.

Use the space here to write about how that feels:

....

....

....

....

....

....

....

....

....

....

....

....

....

....

....

....

....

....

....

....

....

4.   Jiggle

Sit, stand, or lie down and start jiggling your body. No rules; just shake it, baby. Try a consistent jiggle for 60 seconds. See what happens. Because the body is 70% water, the jiggling has a nourishing effect on the body; it helps it to move, energize, and release the entire system. Take a peek at myofascialrelease.com to read about the jiggling technique called rebounding and its therapeutic effects.

Use the space here to write about how that feels:

....

....

....

....

....

....

....

....

....

....

....

....

....

....

....

....

5. Feel your mug

During your morning cup of tea or coffee ritual, slow down and sip slower. Feel the mug first. What do you notice?

Set a timer for five minutes and write as fast as you can without censoring yourself. I feel _____.

....

....

....

....

....

....

....

....

....

....

....

....

....

....

....

....

....

....

....

6.   Rub your arms or legs with great-smelling lotion

Grab your favorite moisturizing lotion and spend two to three full minutes or more rubbing it into your arms or legs (or both), taking special care to massage it all the way into your skin. Bonus points if you tell your skin how much you love it while you're rubbing! Your body is a miracle. Thank it for everything it's done for you.

Use the space here to write about how that feels:

....

....

....

....

....

....

....

....

....

....

....

....

....

....

....

....

....

....

7. Stretch your arms

Gently stretch your arms in front of you, then to the side, then overhead, and then behind you, making sure to move slowly and purposefully. Breathe as you go. Be grateful for their movement! The shoulder joint is one of the most flexible in the entire body. Notice the way you can move in all directions from your shoulder.

Use the space here to write about how that feels:

....

....

....

....

....

....

....

....

....

....

....

....

....

....

....

....

....

....

8.   Take a bath, shower, or hot tub

Water is a spiritual medium that often helps to wash negative energy away. Take your bath, shower, or hot tub with that intention, paying close attention to the feeling of the water on your body. Imagine the energy that no longer serves you being washed away. And then, when you're done, imagine it being washed down through the drain into the Earth, where it's turned back into nourishing energy.

Use the space here to write about how that feels:

....

....

....

....

....

....

....

....

....

....

....

....

....

....

....

....

9.   Do some earthing

Take off your shoes and socks, find some soft dirt, grass, or sand, and let your feet connect with the earth beneath you. Breathe deeply and focus on the sensations of Earth energy. You can find the book, *Earthing*, on Amazon to take this practice to the next level and learn about the energy exchange that occurs in the body when it comes into contact with the natural substances of the Earth.

Use the space here to write about how that feels:

....

....

....

....

....

....

....

....

....

....

....

....

....

....

....

....

....

....

10. Stretch your back

Sitting or standing, fold forward slowly, one vertebra at a time. Do not allow any pain to occur. If there's any pain, back up a notch and breathe. Relax with each exhale, and allow the release to take you further down. Notice all the sensations.

Use the space here to write about how that feels:

....

....

....

....

....

....

....

....

....

....

....

....

....

....

....

....

....

....

11.   Get some sun

Let the sun shine on your skin for three to five minutes. Close your eyes and feel the warmth and sensations. A daily dose of sunshine is important for your dose of vitamin D, which is an essential nutrient for the body to function well. Those who are sensitive to the sun or have a condition that prevents them from being in direct sunlight will need to supplement in another way. Even opening your blinds to brighten the room on a sunny day will shift the energy in your room.

Use the space here to write about how that feels:

....

....

....

....

....

....

....

....

....

....

....

....

....

....

....

....

12. Dance

Put on your favorite music and dance. Give yourself permission to be silly or sensual. Notice what you feel. And, of course, you don't even need music. Just dance!

Use the space here to write about how that feels:

....

....

....

....

....

....

....

....

....

....

....

....

....

....

....

....

....

....

....

....

13. Stretch your chest

Draw your arms back behind you slowly. Open the chest and heart space gently, and take a deep breath, expanding the ribcage. Do not allow any pain. Your stretch should feel comfortable. Notice what you feel.

Use the space here to write about how that feels:

....

....

....

....

....

....

....

....

....

....

....

....

....

....

....

....

....

....

....

14.   Walk slowly

Take several steps as slowly as you can. Notice what you feel as you slow down. Pay attention to each part of the movement in each part of your body. Do this for at least one minute.

Use the space here to write about how that feels:

....

....

....

....

....

....

....

....

....

....

....

....

....

....

....

....

....

....

....

15.   Shift your posture into a power pose

Stand tall, head up, shoulders back, fists on your hips, and smile. Stay here for at least twenty seconds with a larger-than-average smile on your face. For an extra bonus, say out loud: "I am awesome!" Notice what that feels like. Posture matters and can affect confidence. Use this exercise in other scenarios by noticing what posture your body takes on when others are present.

Use the space here to write about how that feels. What do you notice?

....

....

....

....

....

....

....

....

....

....

....

....

....

....

....

16. Stretch your fingers

Clasp your hands together, interlacing your fingers, and stretch your fingers forward, back, and in circles for sixty seconds. Release and then massage each finger from the base to the tip individually. Notice what you feel. Your fingertips are one part of your body that contains the most nerve endings of any other part (the lips are a close second).

Use the space here to write about how that feels:

....

....

....

....

....

....

....

....

....

....

....

....

....

....

....

....

....

17.   Drink some water

Fill your favorite glass with room-temperature water and drink it slowly. Take your time between sips to take full breaths. Feel the glass in your hand. Notice the color of the glass and water. Allow yourself to feel the water as it touches your lips, tongue, and throat. Notice what you sense.

Use the space here to write about how that feels:

....

....

....

....

....

....

....

....

....

....

....

....

....

....

....

....

....

....

18. Smile

Smile as wide and as big as you can for no reason. Stay that way for sixty seconds. Smiling has been shown to shift energy and mood. Even a half-grin will do at first.

Use the space here to write about how that feels:

....

....

....

....

....

....

....

....

....

....

....

....

....

....

....

....

....

....

....

....

19.   Open your mouth wide

Make an "O" shape with your mouth as wide as you can without pain. Now make the motion of "E" or a grin as big as you can. Now do "Ah." Do each for ten seconds. Repeat if you like. Notice what you feel. You can research "Face Yoga" and learn more about this practice!

Use the space here to write about how that feels:

....

....

....

....

....

....

....

....

....

....

....

....

....

....

....

....

....

....

20. Look in the mirror

Look at yourself in the mirror for three minutes. Look into your own eyes. Notice the lines on your face and the shapes and colors of your face, eyes, and skin. Be curious about what you see, like you're looking at a stranger. Notice what you feel. You can research "Mirror Work" to learn more about this powerful therapeutic healing modality.

Use the space here to write about how that feels:

....

....

....

....

....

....

....

....

....

....

....

....

....

....

....

....

....

21. Change your sitting posture

Sit in a chair and allow your back to round or slump. Now sit up tall, arching your low back slightly, feeling the weight of your body on each sit bone. Rock back to the rounded or slumped position. And then back to the arched or upright position. Rock back and forth 5-10 times and notice what you feel. If you sit for your job, varying your position during the day will greatly help your body stay mobile and healthy. Taking breaks to stand and walk is even better.

Use the space here to write about how that feels:

....

....

....

....

....

....

....

....

....

....

....

....

....

....

22.   Raise your eyebrows

Go ahead and raise your eyebrows like you're surprised. Hold them there for a second or two, and then relax. Repeat that a few times. See what happens.

Use the space here to write about how that feels:

....

....

....

....

....

....

....

....

....

....

....

....

....

....

....

....

....

....

....

....

23. Shake your booty

Stick that booty out and shake it like nobody's business. This might be a combination of jiggling and dancing. Bonus points for watching yourself in a mirror while you do it. You can call it twerking if you want, but in my day it was, "Shake, shake, shake. . . shake your boo-ty!"

Use the space here to write about how that feels:

....

....

....

....

....

....

....

....

....

....

....

....

....

....

....

....

....

....

24. Wiggle your toes

If it's warm out and you can stick your toes in the grass or sand, do it. But if you don't have the weather or the surface for it, just wiggle wherever you are. Feel the toes in your shoes, on the carpet, or anywhere you happen to be. See if you can wiggle for a full 30 seconds. What do you feel? You can research "Yoga Toes" for a great therapeutic tool that helps stretch the toes and feet and helps prevent bunions and neuroma (foot nerve pain).

Use the space here to write about how that feels:

....

....

....

....

....

....

....

....

....

....

....

....

....

....

....

25.   Pick up grapes (or marbles) with your feet

Sit in a chair, take your shoes off, and place a few grapes on a towel in front of you. You might even find a friend and make this a game of who can pick up the most grapes (or marbles) and put them into a bowl in 60 seconds. Please toss the grapes when you're done. Toe jam and grapes are not very appetizing. This exercise brings you into your body and improves hip, knee, ankle, foot, and toe strength and dexterity.

Use the space here to write about how that feels:

....

....

....

....

....

....

....

....

....

....

....

....

....

....

....

26. Have a massage

Schedule a massage and makes sure you have nowhere to be afterward. Take extra time to clear your mind and feel every stroke. Practice staying present with the sensations in your body. When you have a chance, journal a little bit about what you feel.

Use the space here to write about how that feels:

....

....

....

....

....

....

....

....

....

....

....

....

....

....

....

....

....

....

27. Stretch your hips

Choose your favorite hip stretch and set a timer for three minutes. Breathe, hold, and relax into the stretch until the timer goes off. Release your body a little more with each exhale. How do you feel? You can research "Best hip stretches" or look at some yoga poses for ideas. The hips are intimately related to your low back, so if you have tightness or pain in your back, stretching your hips can help immensely.

Use the space here to write about how that feels:

....

....

....

....

....

....

....

....

....

....

....

....

....

....

....

....

....

28. Hug someone

Count to twenty in your head while you give someone you love a hug. Don't let go until you get to twenty. And if they haven't let go at that point, keep going! Thinking about the love or gratitude you feel for that person while you're hugging is a bonus! If there's no one around to hug, wrap your arms around yourself, or just close your eyes and imagine the hug.

Use the space here to write about how that feels:

....

....

....

....

....

....

....

....

....

....

....

....

....

....

....

....

....

29.   Stretch your lower legs

Your legs do so much for you! The muscles there can hold a lot of tension. Set a timer for 60 seconds and do a little calf stretching or massaging of the lower legs, some on each side. Remember to breathe!

Use the space here to write about how that feels:

....

....

....

....

....

....

....

....

....

....

....

....

....

....

....

....

....

....

....

....

30. Wrap yourself in a heated (or weighted) blanket

This is nice in the winter when you need a little extra warmth. And if you've never tried a weighted blanket, they're particularly amazing. Close your eyes and breathe deeply for at least five minutes. How do you feel?

Use the space here to write about how that feels:

....

....

....

....

....

....

....

....

....

....

....

....

....

....

....

....

....

....

....

....

31. Notice what you smell

Take a moment to notice what you smell. Close your eyes and focus on any smells in the room. Take a moment to write about it. If there are no significant smells to smell, imagine one of your favorites. Smell is one of the most intense activities in regard to brain activity. Memories are often anchored by smells.

Use the space here to write about how that feels:

....

....

....

....

....

....

....

....

....

....

....

....

....

....

....

....

....

....

32. Make a funny sound

Try a squawk or a gobble. Or maybe a high-pitched opera-like noise. Any sound will do. If you have learned how to chant, go ahead and "OM." Repeat it ten times. If you're brave, sing a song, like for real. Look up the lyrics online and sing the whole thing. How do you feel?

Use the space here to write about how that feels:

....

....

....

....

....

....

....

....

....

....

....

....

....

....

....

....

....

....

33. Go swimming or float

Take a little outing to your neighborhood pool and swim, walk in the water, or float. If a pool isn't in the cards, a bath, maybe? Even a shower will do! Remember, water is a spiritual medium. Spend some moments feeling the water on your skin, the temperature of the water and your body, and the sensation of energy throughout your body.

Use the space here to write about how that feels:

....
....
....
....
....
....
....
....
....
....
....
....
....
....
....
....
....

34. Notice what you hear inside the room

Take a moment to close your eyes and notice what you hear. Even in a quiet room, you may find that you can hear things you never noticed before when you tune in. Spend 3-5 minutes focused on what you hear. Write about it. A shift to what you hear can quickly shift your attention, energy, and mood.

Use the space here to write about how that feels:

....

....

....

....

....

....

....

....

....

....

....

....

....

....

....

....

....

....

35.   Notice what you hear outside

Go outside and tune into what you hear. If you can safely close your eyes, do so, and focus on the sounds. Is it a bird? A plane? A car? Children playing? Just breathe and notice.

Use the space here to write about how that feels:

....

....

....

....

....

....

....

....

....

....

....

....

....

....

....

....

....

....

....

36. Give yourself a face massage

You can use a couple of fingers and a circular motion. Try spending at least 2-3 minutes massaging the forehead, temples, nose, cheeks, jawline, and ears; anything that feels good! You might even pair this with a great cleanser at night before you go to bed. What do you notice after you're done? Also, remember, in eastern medicine philosophy, the ears have points corresponding to every part of the body. It might be fun to look up the points on an auricular (ear) acupuncture chart to see which places correspond to which body parts and focus. The same goes for the hands and feet, by the way.

Use the space here to write about how that feels:

....
....
....
....
....
....
....
....
....
....
....
....
....
....

37. Finger paint

Find some paper, and you can order finger-paints, or you can use another substance (like mud or pudding). Anything goes. This is about touch and sensation. Can you feel it? When you have a chance, journal about the sensations and experience.

Use the space here to write about how that feels:

....

....

....

....

....

....

....

....

....

....

....

....

....

....

....

....

....

....

38. Treat yourself to a mud mask

Look up some natural concoctions, or buy a pre-made mask at the drug store. Take your time applying the mask, then set a timer for 15 minutes and focus on meditation or deep breathing while you wait. When it's time to wash it off, move slowly and notice what you feel. Your face will love you for it!

Use the space here to write about how that feels:

....

....

....

....

....

....

....

....

....

....

....

....

....

....

....

....

....

39. Try an essential oil

Put a drop of one of your favorite essential oils into your hands, rub them together and cup them around your nose, and breathe deeply.

Essential oils are powerful medicine. Read up a little on different oils and what they're used for. For a quick pick-me-up, use peppermint. One drop will do, promise! Peppermint is also great for relieving headaches. How do you feel? Other scents can be used for other issues or goals. Lavender is great for relaxation. DoTerra and Young Living are my favorite essential oil companies.

Use the space here to write about how that feels:

....

....

....

....

....

....

....

....

....

....

....

....

....

....

....

40. Legs up the wall pose

Lie on your back with your legs straight up the wall and your arms by your sides. There should be no pain with this position. Breathe deeply while meditating on the sounds in the room. Try this for three minutes and see how you feel. You can also put your legs up over a chair if the wall is too difficult. In Yoga, this pose is called Viparita Karani. Research both the benefits and the contraindications of all Yoga poses before you partake.

Use the space here to write about how that feels:

....
....
....
....
....
....
....
....
....
....
....
....
....
....
....
....
....

41.   Sway side to side

You can do this sitting or standing. Notice the feeling of shifting your weight from side to side. What can you feel? Try for 60 seconds.

Use the space here to write about how that feels:

....

....

....

....

....

....

....

....

....

....

....

....

....

....

....

....

....

....

....

....

42. Breath of fire

You can research "breath of fire" to get more info on this kind of therapeutic breathing, but for now, breathe in and out of your nose in short bursts for 15 seconds, focusing on the lower belly movement and contraction/relaxation. Notice what you feel.

Use the space here to write about how that feels:

....

....

....

....

....

....

....

....

....

....

....

....

....

....

....

....

....

....

....

....

43. Crawl across the room (or bed)

Crawling is a fun activity that we typically stop doing after we figure out how to walk as a baby. Doing this motion will shift your energy and shake up your body movement in a good way. You can try it forward and backward. What do you notice? Make sure you're crawling on a carpet or softer surface to protect your knees from being scraped. Can't crawl? Even just positioning yourself on your hands and knees can bring you more into your body. You can even do the movement across your bed.

Use the space here to write about how that feels:

....
....
....
....
....
....
....
....
....
....
....
....
....
....

44. Visit your local gym and take a tour

You can just explore and talk to someone new. Ask them to describe the facilities and classes and then ask them a couple of questions. Notice the people in the gym, their bodies, clothes, movements, and expressions. This is more about the connection than joining the gym. Journal about your experience.

Use the space here to write about how that feels:

....

....

....

....

....

....

....

....

....

....

....

....

....

....

....

....

....

....

45. Take a trial class at your local Yoga or Pilates studio

Most yoga studios will allow you to take a trial class. Ask for an appropriate level class for your stage and ability.

Use the space here to write about how that feels:

....
....
....
....
....
....
....
....
....
....
....
....
....
....
....
....
....
....
....
....

46. Make homemade veggie soup

Look up a recipe and make soup. Take your time preparing the veggies. Slow down and enjoy the process of chopping. Notice your energy. The energy you embody while cooking is infused into the food. Add some love! When you're ready to eat the soup, do so mindfully, really taking care to taste each spoonful. Share a container with your neighbor.

Use the space here to write about how that feels:

....

....

....

....

....

....

....

....

....

....

....

....

....

....

....

....

....

47. Take a dance class

In-person or online, either way will be a blast. How did it make you feel?

Use the space here to write about how that feels:

....

....

....

....

....

....

....

....

....

....

....

....

....

....

....

....

....

....

....

....

48. Skip

How long has it been? Give it a try. You can even skip in place while holding onto a sturdy handrail if that feels safer.

Use the space here to write about how that feels:

....

....

....

....

....

....

....

....

....

....

....

....

....

....

....

....

....

....

....

....

49. Hula hoop

You can find them at the dollar store in the summer or online. Spend at least five minutes working that hoop! You can do the traditional version around your waist or swing your hoop around an arm or leg. How did it make you feel?

My friend Amanda DeCarlo, founder of Breath.Dance has some great resources for you. Take a peek at https://www.breath.dance/

Use the space here to write about how that feels:

....

....

....

....

....

....

....

....

....

....

....

....

....

....

....

50. Bounce a ball

Small, medium, or large, get your hands on a ball and bounce it. You can bounce it on the ground or against a wall. Make it a game and see how many times you can bounce it in a row before it gets away from you.

Use the space here to write about how that feels:

....
....
....
....
....
....
....
....
....
....
....
....
....
....
....
....
....
....
....

51. Take a power nap

It's a miracle what a good nap will do for you. My friend Honorée says, "Naps are a success strategy." Feeling tired? It's okay to take that extra nap. Journal a little after you wake, especially if you can remember your dreams.

Use the space here to write about how that feels:

....

....

....

....

....

....

....

....

....

....

....

....

....

....

....

....

....

....

52. Say aloud, "My body knows how to heal."

Affirmations are powerful energy shifters. Choose this one, or make your own version. For bonus points, look in the mirror while you do it! How does this feel? You can also shift your affirmation into an afformation by changing it into a question. For example: "Why does my body always know how to heal itself?" You can research Dr. Noah St. John and his books on afformations to learn more.

Use the space here to write about how that feels:

....
....
....
....
....
....
....
....
....
....
....
....
....
....
....
....
....

53. Lay flat on the floor and breathe

Prop yourself with blankets, towels, pillows, or bolsters for maximum comfort and rest with some deep breathing. Allowing your body to lie flat stretches the hip flexors and the back. If there's any pain, shift your position for comfort. In Yoga, this pose is called Savasana and is the final resting pose in most routines. Set a timer for five minutes and breathe.

Use the space here to write about how that feels:

....
....
....
....
....
....
....
....
....
....
....
....
....
....
....
....
....

54. Schedule some bodywork or a healing session

Different from a massage, try another kind of bodywork: Myofascial release, Zero Balancing, Trigger Point Release, acupuncture—ask for a recommendation and try something new! There are many ways to nourish the body and enhance healing. If you have nothing to heal (no pain or immediate issues), try a session to take your meditation or spiritual practice deeper.

Use the space here to write about how that feels:

....

....

....

....

....

....

....

....

....

....

....

....

....

....

....

....

55. Ride a bike

Yes, a stationary bike counts! Try any bike you can access which is fun and easy! Go for a ten, fifteen, or thirty-minute ride.

Use the space here to write about how that feels:

....
....
....
....
....
....
....
....
....
....
....
....
....
....
....
....
....
....
....
....

56. Body scan meditation

Tara Brach is one of my favorite awareness, body awareness, and meditation teachers. Try her body scan mediation here: https://youtu.be/eDnBVUz3a7Y

Use the space here to write about how that feels:

....

....

....

....

....

....

....

....

....

....

....

....

....

....

....

....

....

....

....

....

57.　Inhabit the body talk

Here's one more. Listen to this meditation by Tara Brach about inhabiting the body:

https://www.tarabrach.com/meditation-inhabiting-body/

Use the space here to write about how what came to you:

....

....

....

....

....

....

....

....

....

....

....

....

....

....

....

....

....

....

58. Stay warm

Especially for the days of the year when you can feel your body reacting to the cold; stay extra diligent about a warm blanket, bath, food and drinks, and clothes. Keeping your hands and feet warm will help your whole body. A few minutes of vigorous exercise will increase your body temperature too. You can research temperature as it relates to health by looking for information on acupuncture or eastern medicine philosophies.

Use the space here to write about what it feels like to be warm:

....

....

....

....

....

....

....

....

....

....

....

....

....

....

....

59. Journal about a body part that you're grateful for

Choose one of the body parts you love and write a love letter to it.

Use the space below to write:

....

....

....

....

....

....

....

....

....

....

....

....

....

....

....

....

....

....

....

....

60. Write down everything awesome that your body has accomplished

Your body is an amazing miracle. Do a little journaling in list form about everything it has done and can do. If you can breathe [wink], start with that. List them all.

Use the space below for your list:

....

....

....

....

....

....

....

....

....

....

....

....

....

....

....

....

....

....

....

61. Close your eyes and watch the back of your eyelids

Sit in a comfortable position and soften your eyes, gently closing them. Begin to focus on the back of your eyelids with your eyes closed. Breathe gently and notice any sensations. What do you see as you gently focus?

Use the space here to write about how that feels:

....

....

....

....

....

....

....

....

....

....

....

....

....

....

....

....

....

....

....

62. Play hopscotch

Grab some chalk from the dollar store and create your grid. If this feels too complicated, you can even try just standing on one leg next to the kitchen counter and noticing what you feel.

Use the space here to write about how that feels:

....

....

....

....

....

....

....

....

....

....

....

....

....

....

....

....

....

....

....

....

63. Kiss

Either real or imagined you will feel some goodness, I promise. You can give your cat or dog a kiss, or you can give your own self a kiss. The fingertips and the lips are the two places in the body with the most nerve endings!

Use the space here to write about how that feels

....

....

....

....

....

....

....

....

....

....

....

....

....

....

....

....

....

....

64. Hold hands

The next time you get a chance, grab someone's hand and squeeze a bit. Notice the sensation of the grip, their response, the temperature, etc. If you don't have someone's hand to hold, place both hands over your chest, one on top of the other, and pause to breathe. Allow the gentle weight of your hands over the chest to be your focus. Mediate on all the sensations.

Use the space here to write about how that feels:

....
....
....
....
....
....
....
....
....
....
....
....
....
....
....
....
....
....

65. Wear a pair of really comfy slippers

Happy feet are an amazing thing. Slide on your slippers and feel how they feel against your feet. Take a few steps and notice the cushion under your feet and how your feet move inside the slipper. If you don't own a comfy pair, maybe it's time to go shopping!

Use the space here to write about how that feels:

....

....

....

....

....

....

....

....

....

....

....

....

....

....

....

....

....

....

66. Say out loud to yourself, "My body feels strong and flexible," and flex your bicep a little bit

Notice how it feels to say that out loud. Bonus for looking in the mirror while you do it. What do you notice?

Use the space here to write about how that feels:

....

....

....

....

....

....

....

....

....

....

....

....

....

....

....

....

....

....

....

....

67.   Knead some dough

You can use Playdough or real dough for this exercise. How does it feel in your hands? What do you notice? Knead for at least a minute or so. If you're making bread, or pizza crust (my favorite), take extra care to slow down during this process and put a few love vibes into your creation.

Use the space here to write about how that feels:

....

....

....

....

....

....

....

....

....

....

....

....

....

....

....

....

....

68. Spend five minutes rubbing some lotion into your hands

Grab your favorite hand lotion and spend a good five minutes giving yourself a hand massage, making sure to pay attention to each finger and all the crevices in between. Massage each web space between the fingers, and around each bone of the hand (metacarpals). Notice the veins, freckles, or other marks or wrinkles around your knuckles. Send some gratitude into your hands.

Use the space here to write about how that feels:

....

....

....

....

....

....

....

....

....

....

....

....

....

....

....

69. Have an acupuncture session

Acupuncture is one of my favorite healing modalities because of the increased energy flow for all body systems. You can also research "acupressure points" for many ailments and issues. But if you have access to an acupuncturist, try a session with a professional.

Use the space here to write about how you felt after the session:

....

....

....

....

....

....

....

....

....

....

....

....

....

....

....

....

....

70. Buy and wear a great-fitting pair of jeans

Notice how great-fitting jeans feel on your body. Pay attention to how you move in them and how they feel around your waist and legs. Notice how the material feels on your skin and the connection of the material to different areas of your hips, thighs, and lower legs. Great-fitting clothes will shift your energy and mood and help you feel more confident. If you want to take your clothing to another level, hire a stylist to help you with a few new outfits this season!

Use the space here to write about how that feels:

....
....
....
....
....
....
....
....
....
....
....
....
....
....
....

71.   Spend five minutes in child's pose

One of the most relaxing Yoga poses is child's pose. You can research the pose first if you're unfamiliar with it. If it's hard on your knees, use pillows under your hips. And place a small, rolled-up towel in front of you as a headrest. Ease into the pose and notice how your body feels as it relaxes into the pose. Try to hold for 2-5 minutes. Mediate and focus on your breathing.

Use the space here to write about how that feels:

....

....

....

....

....

....

....

....

....

....

....

....

....

....

....

....

72. Try gyan mudra

Mudras are hand positions used to purify and direct energy flow in your mind and body. Look up and practice the hand position, Gyan mudra. The literal translation is 'mudra of wisdom and knowledge.' This hand pose or position is known to be one of the most prominent to support better mental and physical health. The pose is performed by touching the thumb to the index finger, with the third, fourth, and pinky fingers all straight alongside each other and touching.

Use the space below to write about how this feels. What do you notice?

....
....
....
....
....
....
....
....
....
....
....
....
....
....
....

73. Practice a self-myofascial release technique of your choosing

Go to www.MyofascialRelease.com and look up one of the self-releases. Spend at least five minutes with the technique.

Use the space below to write about how this feels. What do you notice?

....

....

....

....

....

....

....

....

....

....

....

....

....

....

....

....

....

....

....

74. Unclench your jaw

Close your eyes and bring your attention to your jaw. Relax and unclench. Allow the tongue to rest on the roof of the mouth while the lips are closed and the teeth are slightly parted. This is considered the resting position of the TMJ (tempomandibular joint) or jaw. Rest for several deep breaths.

Use the space below to write about how this feels. What do you notice?

....

....

....

....

....

....

....

....

....

....

....

....

....

....

....

....

....

75. Use an extra pillow behind your back when you sit

If you sit for a living, most times, you're so focused on work that you forget you have a body. Give your back some attention by placing a soft-but-firm extra pillow or cushion behind your back. Allow your back and body to rest on the cushion. A great cushion will support the natural lumbar (low back) curve and help keep your spine healthy. Take a few breaths.

Use the space below to write about how this feels. What do you notice?

....

....

....

....

....

....

....

....

....

....

....

....

....

....

....

76. Say aloud, "I feel so energized today!"

Another great affirmation! Say it out loud and see how you feel. You can turn this one into an afformation by converting it into a powerful question: Why do I feel so energized today?

Use the space below to write about how this feels. What do you notice?

....

....

....

....

....

....

....

....

....

....

....

....

....

....

....

....

....

....

....

77. Try prana mudra (for happiness)

Here's a hand posture or pose you can have fun with, meant to bring happiness. Mudras are hand positions used to purify and direct energy flow in your mind and body. The prana mudra is performed by bringing the tips of the ring and little finger together with the thumb. Take several deep breaths while holding this hand position. This is the mudra for life force or happiness.

Use the space below to write about how this feels. What do you notice?

....

....

....

....

....

....

....

....

....

....

....

....

....

....

....

78.   Take a restorative yoga class

There are many kinds of Yoga classes, but restorative (yin) Yoga is one of the best for helping you into your body for nourishment and healing. You can take a class or research "restorative yoga poses" to find something you can try.

Use the space below to write about how this feels. What do you notice?

....

....

....

....

....

....

....

....

....

....

....

....

....

....

....

....

....

....

79. Stand in mountain pose for five minutes

Maybe you're noticing the Yoga theme here? While I'm not a huge yogini, I love to use body positions as awareness portals. Mountain pose is standing with your feet about shoulder-width apart, arms by the sides, posture tall and aligned, ears over the shoulders, and shoulders over the hips. Breathe and feel the energy of the Earth moving up through your feet. Ground and center yourself in this pose by feeling your connection to the Earth.

Use the space below to write about how this feels. What do you notice?

....

....

....

....

....

....

....

....

....

....

....

....

....

....

....

....

80. Scalp massage

A great self-scalp massage will energize you for the rest of the day. Whether you're treating yourself or being treated, notice the pressure of the fingertips on the scalp. Pay attention to all areas of the head, from the base of the neck to the top, where your hairline meets your forehead. Follow the hairline to where it meets the sides of your head over your ears. You're bringing energy and flow to the hair, scalp, and cranial bones underneath your fingers.

Use the space below to write about how this feels. What do you notice?

....

....

....

....

....

....

....

....

....

....

....

....

....

....

....

....

....

81.   Eat all organic for one day

Maybe you're already treating your body to organic, whole food. But if you've been slacking, try it for a day and see how your system responds with increased energy. If your diet has been poor (high sugar, processed foods), beware; you'll need to add whole, natural, organic food slowly, paying attention to how your body reacts. This can be detoxification for your system, and you may need some professional guidance. My friend Dr. Elle is a wonderful resource. Find her programs at https://www.wellspringnaturalhealthinstitute.com

Eating whole organic food brings you back to a connection with the Earth—it's powerful medicine.

Use the space below to write about how this feels. What do you notice?

....

....

....

....

....

....

....

....

....

....

....

....

....

82. Feel your heartbeat

Place one hand over the left side of your chest, over your heart. Connect with a few deep breaths and feel the beat of your heart. Mediate on that sensation for one to three minutes or more if you're able.

Use the space below to write about how this feels. What do you notice?

....

....

....

....

....

....

....

....

....

....

....

....

....

....

....

....

....

....

....

83. Hold a baby

I realize not all of you may have access, but if you do, ask to hold a baby and revel in their energy. If it's your own baby, take extra care to feel, see, smell, hear, and taste your baby. A small kiss will do for the taste part! Babies have amazing energy. Allow yourself to receive it.

Use the space below to write about how this feels. What do you notice?

....

....

....

....

....

....

....

....

....

....

....

....

....

....

....

....

....

....

84. Pet your cat or dog

There is science showing the positive benefits of petting your pet. The activity lowers the stress hormone, cortisol and increases the level of the feel-good hormone, oxytocin. When you take this on as a vibe-shifting activity, bring your attention and intention to the energy with which you approach, touch, and pet your pet. Allow yourself to receive the good vibes back from them. Animals are sacred creatures that can act as a window to your soul.

Use the space below to write about how this feels. What do you notice?

....
....
....
....
....
....
....
....
....
....
....
....
....
....
....

85.   Eat or drink some superfood

Superfoods (look them up) have increased amounts of nutrients and antioxidants. Some examples are soy, blueberries, salmon, green tea, walnuts, broccoli, and spinach. Make a focused effort to choose one today and complete a mindful eating exercise with it. Take time to notice how the food looks and smells before you taste it. What is its texture? Make eating all your food a mindful experience, and get ready to transform your food routine.

Use the space below to write about how this feels. What do you notice?

....

....

....

....

....

....

....

....

....

....

....

....

....

....

....

....

86. Sleep in

When was the last time you allowed yourself to sleep in without an alarm clock blasting you out of dreamland? Purposefully choose a day when you don't have to rise with an alarm, craft a going-to-bed ritual (you'll find some amazing resources from my friend Kelly Myerson at https://beingwellwithkelly.com/get-your-best-sleep-ever/), and then plan on sleeping as long as you want to the next morning. When you do wake, take several moments to bask in gratitude, eyes still closed, before you get out of bed.

Use the space below to write about how this feels. What do you notice?

....
....
....
....
....
....
....
....
....
....
....
....
....
....
....

87.   Practice a body scrub or skin brushing

I learned the dry brushing technique when I completed a detox program with my friend Neelam Singh (find some great resources on her page here: https://www.momentinspired.com/). Not only will dry brushing stimulate circulation, but it'll also help you move into your body almost immediately. You can use a loofah or even make homemade body scrubs. Plan a day when you can spend some extra time with this technique during your morning routine. Notice what you feel as you spend time over each area of your body.

Use the space below to write about how this feels. What do you notice?

....

....

....

....

....

....

....

....

....

....

....

....

....

....

88. Do some kundalini yoga

kun·da·li·ni

/ ˌko͞ondə ˈlēnē/

noun

1.   (in yoga) latent female energy believed to lie coiled at the base of the spine.

• A system of meditation directed toward the release of kundalini energy. noun: **kundalini yoga**

Try this basic kundalini movement to enhance kundalini energy in your body: The cactus pose: Place your arms up in the air at right angles, like the shape of a cactus, opening up the chest and keeping the head and neck posture tall. Inhale through the nose as you rotate your whole trunk to the left. Exhale through the mouth while rotating the whole trunk to the right. Repeat three to five times.

Use the space below to write about how this feels. What do you notice?

....

....

....

....

....

....

....

....

....

....

89. Pleasure yourself sexually

"Your sexuality is tied intimately to your creativity. If one is blocked, the other is blocked." I remember a coach helping me understand this idea, which was transformational for me. Rather than trying to give you any particular technique (because a hot bath can be 'sensual'), you'll find some amazing resources from an author friend of mine, Erika Delauney, here: https://desirealchemy.com/

Once you choose an activity, protect some private time and spend it with yourself.

Use the space below to write about what you notice.

....
....
....
....
....
....
....
....
....
....
....
....
....
....
....

90. Go to a department store and test perfumes

If you dislike perfume smells, do a version of this exercise in the produce department of a grocery store with the fruit or flowers. The idea is to engage your olfactory senses and notice what you sense. Try three or four different smells. Notice your reactions to each smell. Does anything trigger a memory?

Use the space below to write about this. What do you notice?

....

....

....

....

....

....

....

....

....

....

....

....

....

....

....

....

....

....

91. Swing on a swing

How long has it been? Is there a neighborhood park you could walk to that has swings? Take a moment to sit and swing gently. And then, if you're adventurous, see how high you can swing! Notice all the sensations.

Use the space below to write about this. What do you notice?

....

....

....

....

....

....

....

....

....

....

....

....

....

....

....

....

....

....

92. Build a sandcastle

Even a walk on the beach will do. But if you can park yourself in that spot between the damp and dry sand, and build a castle, even better. Notice what you feel, hear, smell, taste, and see. Take your time. Enjoy the sensations. Small, medium, or large, any size castle will do!

Use the space below to write about this. What do you notice?

....
....
....
....
....
....
....
....
....
....
....
....
....
....
....
....
....
....

93. Walk in a labyrinth

You may have to ask around if you don't know where to find one, but some neighborhood churches or spiritual centers have labyrinths. They are meant for walking meditation and are tools for personal, psychological, and spiritual transformation. Research their meaning and origin for more info. When you begin your walk, take your time. Clear your mind and make every step a mindful one. What do you notice?

Use the space below to write about what you noticed.

....
....
....
....
....
....
....
....
....
....
....
....
....
....
....
....
....

94. Go hiking

This is a slightly more intense commitment than a neighborhood walk. Find a trail to hike and enjoy the different scenery. Notice the sights, smells, sounds, and feels. If your mind drifts, attempt to bring your awareness back to your breath and what you're sensing.

Use the space below to write about this. What did you notice?

....
....
....
....
....
....
....
....
....
....
....
....
....
....
....
....
....
....
....
....

95. Stomp your feet

This activity is best done with good, cushioned shoes and a softer surface for stomping. Notice how it feels to stomp. Try it three times. Pause and take notice. Try it again. What do you feel?

Use the space below to write about this. What did you notice?

....

....

....

....

....

....

....

....

....

....

....

....

....

....

....

....

....

....

96. Snap your fingers to your favorite song

You may be surprised how challenging snapping is if you haven't done it in a while. Don't attach to the perfect snap. Just give it a try for a minute or so. Then up-level your practice by putting on one of your favorite dance songs and snapping to the beat.

Use the space below to write about this. What did you notice?

....
....
....
....
....
....
....
....
....
....
....
....
....
....
....
....
....
....
....

97. Rub your earlobes

This is surprisingly very therapeutic, probably because of the acupressure points associated with relaxation around the ear. Try it for 60 seconds and see how you feel.

Use the space below to write about this. What do you notice?

....

....

....

....

....

....

....

....

....

....

....

....

....

....

....

....

....

....

....

....

98. Jump

You can try many great variations of this, including jumping a couple of inches with two feet in place, jumping from one location to the next with two feet or with one foot leading, jumping on a trampoline, or jumping rope. Try it once, a few times, or for 30-60 seconds. This is surprisingly quite a workout, so pace yourself. What do you notice? Not physically able to jump? Close your eyes and imagine it for 60 seconds.

Use the space below to write about this. What do you notice?

....
....
....
....
....
....
....
....
....
....
....
....
....
....
....

99. Eat something you have to suck on first

Whether it's a lollipop, Werther's Original, Jolly Rancher, Gobstopper, or your thumb, enjoy the sensation of sucking on something. If your mind wanders to something sexual, so be it. The point here is to slow down and notice what you taste.

Use the space below to write about this. What do you notice?

....

....

....

....

....

....

....

....

....

....

....

....

....

....

....

....

....

....

100. Try a foam roller

There are many forms of bodywork tools you can use to perform self-myofascial release and stretches. Choose your favorite tool and one body part that could use extra love and attention. Spend three to five minutes on that body area, maintaining gentle pressure with breathing and relaxation.

Use the space below to write about this. What do you notice? Fill in the blank: I feel _____.

....

....

....

....

....

....

....

....

....

....

....

....

....

....

....

....

....

....

PART TWO

GOOD VIBES
FOR YOUR MIND

When you use and master your mind, you have another powerful way to shift your vibe. Your mind can drive your emotions and behaviors. Almost everything starts in the mind. Here are some simple ways to raise your vibration using the power of your mind.

101. Notice the temperature in the room

Stop, get still, and notice the temperature in the room. What are you thinking when you notice how warm or cold it is?

Use the space below to write. When I think about the temperature:

....

....

....

....

....

....

....

....

....

....

....

....

....

....

....

....

....

....

....

102. Imagine a campfire

Close your eyes and stare into the flames. What do you see?
Use the space below to write. The flames make me feel:

....

....

....

....

....

....

....

....

....

....

....

....

....

....

....

....

....

....

....

....

....

103. Be aware of what you feel

You are not your body. You are the consciousness that notices your body. Take a step back from everything and notice it all. What do you sense? Who is it that senses?

Take a moment to write. When I notice what I feel:

....
....
....
....
....
....
....
....
....
....
....
....
....
....
....
....
....
....
....
....
....

104. Meditate

I always hesitate to use the "M" word because people have a freakout moment sometimes. Meditation could be noticing how the water feels on your hands when you're doing the dishes. Take five minutes and get still. Breathe and notice what you're feeling and thinking without judging it. It's that simple.

Write about it. When I try to meditate:

....

....

....

....

....

....

....

....

....

....

....

....

....

....

....

....

....

....

105. Remember joy

Take a few breaths and remember a happy moment when you were smiling, laughing, or joyful. Bask there for at least five minutes or more.

Take a moment to write. When I remember joy:

....

....

....

....

....

....

....

....

....

....

....

....

....

....

....

....

....

....

....

....

106. Journal your limiting beliefs

Take a few moments and write down all the limiting thoughts, beliefs, or habitual tapes you hear during the day that tell you you're not good enough. Make a list of them. Then for each one, write a reason why it isn't true.

This one is already a journaling exercise - so feel free to use the space below.

....

....

....

....

....

....

....

....

....

....

....

....

....

....

....

....

....

....

....

107. Write a love letter

Use the space below to choose someone you love and write them a love letter. What do you want them to know? How do you want them to feel?

....

....

....

....

....

....

....

....

....

....

....

....

....

....

....

....

....

....

....

....

....

108. Visualize yourself in your favorite place

They say there is no difference to your brain whether you're actually experiencing something or experiencing it through visualization. So, spend several minutes imagining all the sights, sounds, tastes, smells, and feels of one of your favorite places.

Use the space below to journal. When I'm in my favorite space:

....

....

....

....

....

....

....

....

....

....

....

....

....

....

....

....

....

....

109. Say out loud: "My friends and family support everything I do."

Affirmations like this will usually bring things up for you. You may have thoughts, feelings, or emotions. What are they? Notice how you feel when you say this out loud.

Take a moment to write. When I say this out loud, I feel:

....
....
....
....
....
....
....
....
....
....
....
....
....
....
....
....
....
....
....
....

110. Think about someone you love

Close your eyes and bring someone you love into your mind. Can you picture their face? Their clothes? Their environment? What are they doing or saying? How do they smell? This may bring up emotions. Give yourself permission to feel.

Take a moment to write. When I think about someone I love:

....

....

....

....

....

....

....

....

....

....

....

....

....

....

....

....

111. Dwell in gratitude

There's often no faster way to raise your vibe than gratitude. What are you grateful for? Spend a moment, or as long as you like, basking in the feelings of gratitude.

Take a moment to write. What are you grateful for, and how does that make you feel?

....

....

....

....

....

....

....

....

....

....

....

....

....

....

....

....

....

....

112. Think about what matters to you

Take a moment to ponder the question: What matters to you? What comes into your mind first?

Use the space below to write about it.

....

....

....

....

....

....

....

....

....

....

....

....

....

....

....

....

....

....

....

....

113. What do you love so much you lose track of time?

Use the space below to write about it.

....
....
....
....
....
....
....
....
....
....
....
....
....
....
....
....
....
....
....
....
....
....

114. What is something you could teach?

Use the space below to write about that subject, like you're teaching it to a fifth grader.

....

....

....

....

....

....

....

....

....

....

....

....

....

....

....

....

....

....

....

....

....

....

115. Listen to ocean sounds

Choose a relaxation app or YouTube video that offers an ocean sounds or nature sounds track. Close your eyes and listen to the entire track while focusing on completing deep breaths. What do you notice?

Use the space below to write. When I hear this sound:

....

....

....

....

....

....

....

....

....

....

....

....

....

....

....

....

....

....

....

....

116. Listen to any guided meditation

There are many ways to meditate. Today, choose an app or a track on YouTube and listen to the meditation all the way through. Close your eyes and listen to the entire track while focusing on completing deep breaths. What do you notice?

Use the space below to write about what you feel.

....

....

....

....

....

....

....

....

....

....

....

....

....

....

....

....

....

....

117. Listen to Esther (Abraham) Hicks

During one of the most difficult times of my life, when I had the worst time shifting my vibe, I relied on Ester to give me a boost. The way she speaks to us about being the co-creator of our lives is always inspirational and offers a life-changing perspective. Look her up on YouTube and enjoy one of her lectures.

Use the space below to write. What are some of the thoughts or Ahas that came up for you?

....

....

....

....

....

....

....

....

....

....

....

....

....

....

....

....

....

....

118. Say out loud: "Why are my problems all so easy to solve?"

This statement, in the form of a 'why' question, is called an afformation. Dr. Noah St. John teaches us about the brain science of asking questions instead of using statements in his book *Millionaire Afformations*. I loved the palpable shift in energy I felt when I changed many of my affirmation statements to afformation questions. Sometimes an affirmation statement will feel like a reach when you don't really feel that way. But a question feels different. Try it!

Use the space below to write down your afformation. Dr. Noah recommends writing it 15 times to help retrain the mind.

....

....

....

....

....

....

....

....

....

....

....

....

....

....

119. Do some sound healing

Go to www.ListeningtoSmile.com and listen to a sample track. You can also find some of Ian's music on Bandcamp and YouTube. My friend Ian Morris produces music that is vibrationally tuned for different positive effects. Since everything is energy and vibration, listening for as little as ten minutes a day can shift your energy and begin a healing process.

Use the space below to write. What did you feel when you listened?

....

....

....

....

....

....

....

....

....

....

....

....

....

....

....

....

120. Play an instrument

Any instrument will do, even banging a wooden spoon on a pot. But if you have access to a piano, guitar, recorder, triangle, or even a singing bowl, go play. Experiment with the sounds and see what you notice. Try it out for at least five minutes.

Use the space below to write. When I play music, I feel:

....

....

....

....

....

....

....

....

....

....

....

....

....

....

....

....

....

....

121. Admire a garden

Your area of the world might have a special public garden space, a park, or a community playground where you can admire nature. Sit for at least five minutes and notice what you see, hear, taste, smell, and feel. I love Brookside Gardens in the Washington D.C. area.

Use the space below to write. Sitting in the garden makes me feel:

....

....

....

....

....

....

....

....

....

....

....

....

....

....

....

....

....

....

122. Count backward from 100

Many relaxation techniques use counting. It's a quick, easy way to focus on something simple that shifts your energy. It is meditative, keeping you in the moment.

Use the space below to write. Counting made me feel:

....

....

....

....

....

....

....

....

....

....

....

....

....

....

....

....

....

....

....

....

123. Detach from the feeling

When you notice a feeling, practice saying to yourself, "Hmm, that's interesting." Don't make the feeling mean anything. Notice if your mind wanders and starts to add thoughts, beliefs, or meaning to the feeling. Instead, come back to the sensation of the feeling in your body. Breathe and make space for it.

Use the space below to write. When I detach from the meaning of this feeling:

....

....

....

....

....

....

....

....

....

....

....

....

....

....

....

....

....

124. Say out loud: "I feel amazing!"

Alternatively, use the afformation: "Why do I feel so amazing?" What do you notice? Repeat it five times, and then use the space below to write it out ten to fifteen times.

....

....

....

....

....

....

....

....

....

....

....

....

....

....

....

....

....

....

....

125. Write a list of ways you love to feel

Use the space below:

....

....

....

....

....

....

....

....

....

....

....

....

....

....

....

....

....

....

....

....

....

....

....

126. Write a list of power words

Power words help you feel strong, empowered, inspired, joyful, grateful, or generous. Any high-vibe word that turns you on is a great addition to your list. Use the space below to create your list.

....

....

....

....

....

....

....

....

....

....

....

....

....

....

....

....

....

....

....

....

....

127. Practice toning

A similar exercise is also in the body section. Toning is sound healing that you create from the inside out and is a very powerful healing technique. You can start with the "OM" sound and practice once, making the sound as long as you can before taking another breath. Try this three to five times and see what you notice.

Use the space below to write. When I make the sound, I feel:

....

....

....

....

....

....

....

....

....

....

....

....

....

....

....

....

....

128. Learn how to say "I love you" in another language

Learning how to say anything in another language will shift your vibe, but why not "I love you?" Spend a few minutes learning and practicing in the mirror.

Use the space below to write about this experience.

....

....

....

....

....

....

....

....

....

....

....

....

....

....

....

....

....

....

129. Ask: What else is possible?

Whenever I have a day where something's happening that's out of my control or causing me distress, I default to asking this question instead of immediately reacting out of fear. You must practice this because you're often retraining an ingrained habitual reaction. So when the next situation presents itself, see if you can notice, pause the impending reaction, and then ask yourself, "What else is possible?"

Use the space below to journal out the other possible scenarios you can think of.

....
....
....
....
....
....
....
....
....
....
....
....
....
....
....
....

130. Listen to an inspirational podcast

Choose a topic you love and type it into the iTunes Podcasts app. Enjoy an entertaining or educational podcast about a subject you enjoy.

Use the space below to take some notes about your podcast that you want to remember for later.

....

....

....

....

....

....

....

....

....

....

....

....

....

....

....

....

....

....

....

131. Try something new

Try a new hobby or activity you've never done before. The simple act of trying something new that your mind and body don't know how to do yet, will shift your energy. Notice how it feels. Are you immediately berating yourself for not being good at it? Do you have some natural talent for it? What do you notice about your thoughts, either way?

Take a moment to write about the experience below—good, bad, or awesome.

....

....

....

....

....

....

....

....

....

....

....

....

....

....

....

....

....

132. Speed write

Set a timer for five minutes and write as fast as you can about what you see in front of you. Free or automatic writing is an energy shifter. See what you notice about the process.

Use the space below for your exercise:

....

....

....

....

....

....

....

....

....

....

....

....

....

....

....

....

....

....

....

133. Practice detachment

Choose a day to practice detaching from the meaning or outcome of everything. Practice staying in a neutral mind space no matter what. Use breathwork to get you there in challenging moments. See what you notice. When is it easy? When is it hard?

Use the space below to write about this. What did you notice? What ahas did you have?

....

....

....

....

....

....

....

....

....

....

....

....

....

....

....

....

....

....

134. Ask yourself, "Who would I be without this thought?"

Sometimes shaking yourself awake with a question shifts the vibe immediately. We spend a lot of time in default negativity, but at our core, we know who we are in a divine sense. So asking ourselves that question will be a reminder. And with that awareness, we have a choice. We can stay with the current reaction or choose something more aligned.

Use the space below to write your answer to that question.

....

....

....

....

....

....

....

....

....

....

....

....

....

....

....

....

....

135. Visualize yourself on a pristine beach

Spend a few moments at the beach in your mind. What're you doing? What do you see, feel, taste, hear, or smell? Allow yourself to go there and sense it like you're there. Your brain doesn't know the difference between the actual scene and the one in your mind. Give yourself a few good beach vibes.

Use the space below to write. When I'm at the beach, I feel:

....
....
....
....
....
....
....
....
....
....
....
....
....
....
....
....
....
....

136. Read an inspirational story

The Brave Healer Productions books are chock-full of inspirational stories that'll give you life-changing and energy-shifting perspective. Email us at support@LauraDiFranco.com, and I'll send you a free story! Use the subject line: Good Vibes 365 Free eBook. Otherwise, choose one of the books you already own and read one story you know will energize you.

Use the space below to write. When I'm inspired:

....

....

....

....

....

....

....

....

....

....

....

....

....

....

....

....

....

137. Play a board game, cards, or crossword puzzle

Playing a game, cards, crossword puzzle, or smartphone game is a quick way to shift your vibe.

Use the space below to list some of your favorite games.

....

....

....

....

....

....

....

....

....

....

....

....

....

....

....

....

....

....

....

....

138. Write a tiny mission statement

Most people think about mission statements as things you create for your whole life or company. What about trying a "tiny" version? Write a tiny mission statement for your day, week, or even the next hour. Use the space below to write your tiny mission statement.

....

....

....

....

....

....

....

....

....

....

....

....

....

....

....

....

....

....

....

139. Be curious

When your default mindset is "I can't wait to see what happens next," you override fear with curiosity. When can you use this idea to shift into curiosity? This will take some practice, especially if you're feeling triggered or defensive. The next time the opportunity arises, practice being curious instead of reactive.

Use the space below to write. When I'm curious _____.

....
....
....
....
....
....
....
....
....
....
....
....
....
....
....
....
....
....

140. Post a good vibes sticky note

Write down a positive note on a PostIt note and put it where you know you'll see it. One of my favorites is "You look marvelous!" Any note of affirmation will do!

Time to write. What are ten notes of affirmation you could create PostIts for? Use the space below to list them.

....

....

....

....

....

....

....

....

....

....

....

....

....

....

....

....

....

....

....

141. Document your best childhood memory

Take a few moments to think about a childhood memory that makes you smile. Use the space below to write it down. Remember the sights, sounds, smells, tastes, or sensations.

....

....

....

....

....

....

....

....

....

....

....

....

....

....

....

....

....

....

....

....

....

142. Bask in the moment

Esther Hicks taught me to bask. Since then, I've used the present moment to give myself a sweet gift in the middle of a stressful day. All it takes is a few deep breaths, gratitude for those breaths, and some conscious relaxation. Try it for three to five minutes.

Use the space below to write. When I bask, I feel _____.

....

....

....

....

....

....

....

....

....

....

....

....

....

....

....

....

....

....

143. Start a quote notebook

What are some of your favorite quotes? How do they make you feel? Start a special notebook (or note on your smartphone) just for your favorite inspirational quotes. Make sure it's small enough to fit in your purse or pocket so that when you come across a quote that moves you, you can add it to the collection.

Use the space here to start writing a few down.

....

....

....

....

....

....

....

....

....

....

....

....

....

....

....

....

....

....

....

144. Say to yourself out loud: "I am limitless!"

When I started affirming out loud, it first felt silly. I had to check in with that and realized I wasn't used to telling myself these things. I could say them to others, but when I tried to talk to myself like that, I felt weird. It takes practice. Practice is what creates a new, healthier habit. Another version of this one you can try is: Why is my life so limitless?

Use the space here to write about how it makes you feel when you affirm out loud to yourself.

....

....

....

....

....

....

....

....

....

....

....

....

....

....

....

....

145. Read your favorite magazine cover to cover

How long has it been since you've relaxed with your favorite magazine? One of my favorites is Bella Grace. I also love The Edge Magazine and The On Purpose Woman Magazine, both digital. Find a page, article, or photo that inspires you and spend a few minutes with the feeling of that inspiration. Where is it in your body? Why are you inspired?

Use the space here to write about that feeling of inspiration.

....

....

....

....

....

....

....

....

....

....

....

....

....

....

....

....

....

146. Call out your self-sabotaging thoughts and flip your switch

This is a simple awareness exercise. Take a moment to ponder how much time you spend thinking negative thoughts versus positive. Since you create your tomorrow right this moment, begin to ask yourself: what's a better way to think right now?

Use the space below to call out some of the inner critic thoughts that come up on a regular basis and then flip them to positive affirmations. Write the new affirmations down next.

....
....
....
....
....
....
....
....
....
....
....
....
....
....
....
....

147. Work for a few minutes on a passion project

This book is one of my passion projects. It was written, little by little, over a year or more. I could complete it in small moments of my day when I had no distractions and could sit and write. What's one of your passion projects? Could you take five minutes to focus on it today? And if you don't have any passion projects right now, use the five minutes to meditate on the feeling of passion.

Use the space below to brainstorm your passion project or how the meditation felt.

....
....
....
....
....
....
....
....
....
....
....
....
....
....
....
....

148. Check out the *Mindful - Grateful - Joyful* YouTube channel and listen to a meditation

Use the space below to write about how you felt afterward or about anything that came up.

....

....

....

....

....

....

....

....

....

....

....

....

....

....

....

....

....

....

....

....

149. Download the Insight Timer app on your phone and listen to a meditation

When you have several tools for shifting your vibe, your toolbox becomes that of a master craftsperson. Try this one and use the space below to write your thoughts about how you liked it.

....

....

....

....

....

....

....

....

....

....

....

....

....

....

....

....

....

....

....

....

150. Go to www.TransformationMeditation.com and download a meditation (click the "Free for You" tab)

Here's another meditation site to try! Use the space below to journal your thoughts afterward.

....

....

....

....

....

....

....

....

....

....

....

....

....

....

....

....

....

....

....

....

151. Find a free Knower meditation at https://www.knower.ca/ and listen to one

When you find the right meditation for you, the entire world opens up to possibility. Enhance your toolbox with different versions and see which you love the most.

Use the space below to write about how this one made you feel or about anything that came up.

....

....

....

....

....

....

....

....

....

....

....

....

....

....

....

....

....

....

152. Start writing a book

Open up a new document on your computer and title it: My Book. Then begin by writing your dedication. There, you started writing a book! Don't attach to what this is. Just have fun starting to write today.

Use the space below to outline your thoughts or what came up.

....

....

....

....

....

....

....

....

....

....

....

....

....

....

....

....

....

....

....

153. Set a timer for five minutes and write as fast as you can without censoring yourself:

I love to feel _____.

Writing about what you love to feel is part of my love list journaling. What are all the feelings you enjoy having? Do you love some more than others? Why?

Use the space below to journal.

....

....

....

....

....

....

....

....

....

....

....

....

....

....

....

....

....

....

154. Say out loud to yourself, "I can do this!"

Here's another out-loud affirmation you can try. It will change your energy to move the vibration of your voice from your heart to your tongue. What do you notice?

Use the space below to write about this. Start your writing with the same words: I can do this:

....

....

....

....

....

....

....

....

....

....

....

....

....

....

....

....

....

....

155. Visualize yourself around a campfire on a perfect summer evening with your friends

I love this visualization. What do you see, hear, smell, taste (s'mores, of course), and feel? Set a timer for five minutes and get into the sensations of it. What's cool about your brain is that it doesn't know the difference between experiencing and visualizing something. This is part of the art of manifesting.

Use the space below to write about what came up or the most powerful part of the exercise for you.

....

....

....

....

....

....

....

....

....

....

....

....

....

....

....

....

156. Have a session with a life coach

Have you ever tried this? I used to think I didn't need a life coach because my life was pretty good. I changed my outlook and asked myself: What else could be possible for my life? Then I decided to have fun and try a session. It was life-changing.

Write about how it makes you feel to think about this. What advice or support would you give yourself if you were your own life coach? What questions would you ask yourself?

....

....

....

....

....

....

....

....

....

....

....

....

....

....

....

....

....

157. Place your hands in Namaste for sixty seconds

This is a physical (body) movement, but I'd like you to try to focus on what happens mentally when you do it. What do you notice?

Use the space below to write about it.

....
....
....
....
....
....
....
....
....
....
....
....
....
....
....
....
....
....
....
....
....

158. Ponder the meaning of life

Some of us do this naturally and have spent many hours pondering. Some of us haven't given ourselves a chance to. Today, spend five minutes journaling about the meaning of life.

Use the space below.

....

....

....

....

....

....

....

....

....

....

....

....

....

....

....

....

....

....

159. Google "Binaural Beats" and listen to a track

My friend Ian has some cool versions at listeningtosmile.com for you.

Use the space here to write about how it made you feel.

....

....

....

....

....

....

....

....

....

....

....

....

....

....

....

....

....

....

....

....

....

....

160. Be a great listener for someone who's having a hard time

When I shift my focus to someone else, I shift my energy and focus. It's one of the best ways to shift your vibe. Is there someone in your life you know is struggling? Give them a call or a text today and ask them if they'd like to chat. Practice being a gentle, present ear.

Use the space below to write about how that made you feel or anything that came up.

....

....

....

....

....

....

....

....

....

....

....

....

....

....

....

....

161. Lay off social media and meditate instead

If you find yourself stuck in the scroll, notice how that's making you feel, then close the laptop and push back from your desk. Close your eyes and meditate on the breath for five minutes instead.

Use the space here to write about what you noticed.

....

....

....

....

....

....

....

....

....

....

....

....

....

....

....

....

....

....

162. Make a house of cards

I remember doing this as a kid. Grab a deck of cards and find a study, flat table so you can begin building your castle of cards.

Use the space below to write about what you noticed.

....
....
....
....
....
....
....
....
....
....
....
....
....
....
....
....
....
....
....
....

163. Make a list of your past achievements

Every small, medium, or large thing you've accomplished is something to celebrate. Make an entire list of these and use the list on a day when you feel less accomplished. Notice the pattern.

Use the space below to journal your list.

....

....

....

....

....

....

....

....

....

....

....

....

....

....

....

....

....

....

....

....

164. Go to www.mindmovies.com and watch one

Use the space below to write about what came up for you.

....

....

....

....

....

....

....

....

....

....

....

....

....

....

....

....

....

....

....

....

....

....

....

165. Listen to music recorded at 528 Hz, the vibration of love, peace, and health

My friend Ian has some at listeningtosmile.com

....

....

....

....

....

....

....

....

....

....

....

....

....

....

....

....

....

....

....

....

....

....

166. Look up *PowerThoughts Meditation Club* on YouTube and listen to a meditation

Use the space below to write about what came up for you.

....
....
....
....
....
....
....
....
....
....
....
....
....
....
....
....
....
....
....
....
....
....
....

167. Read the book, *Breaking the Habit of Being Yourself* by Dr. Joe Dispenza

I loved this book, and Dr. Joe has several practical journaling exercises for you to try. Pick your favorite!

....

....

....

....

....

....

....

....

....

....

....

....

....

....

....

....

....

....

....

....

....

168. Remember not to be so serious

There are times in my day when I'll stop and think, *why does everything have to be so serious all the time?* It's, *seriously,* a great question to ask! With awareness, you have a choice. You can choose to lighten up today.

What do you notice when you shift from 'serious' to 'lighter'? Use the space here to write.

....
....
....
....
....
....
....
....
....
....
....
....
....
....
....
....
....
....
....

169. Set a timer for five minutes and write as fast as you can without censoring yourself

The thing that matters the most is _____.

The big questions always turn me on because they are powerful mind and energy shifters. This is about your priorities. What comes up? Use the space below to journal.

....

....

....

....

....

....

....

....

....

....

....

....

....

....

....

....

....

....

....

170. Tour a local museum

It had been a while since I did this, and then my friend Stephanie took us to the Frida Kahlo museum in Mexico during a week retreat there, and I realized how inspiring museums could be. What do you have locally? Use the space below to journal about the piece that inspires you the most. How did it make you feel?

....

....

....

....

....

....

....

....

....

....

....

....

....

....

....

....

....

....

171. Attend a murder mystery or find-your-way-out dinner

These events are fun for so many reasons. But the big point for this is: try something new. There are a million things to try in this world. What do you want to try? Doing something new is a huge energy shifter—even if it's collecting rocks from the nearby stream and painting inspiring words on them (one of my favorite things to do, by the way).

Use the space below to write about how trying something new made you feel.

....

....

....

....

....

....

....

....

....

....

....

....

....

....

....

....

PART THREE

GOOD VIBES FOR YOUR SOUL

All good vibes nourish your soul, but when you connect with your soul regularly, you have another powerful way to shift your vibe. Your soul knows what feels good, what it wants, and what brings you joy. Are you listening? Connecting to your soul will be your GPS for the most aligned, incredible life. Here are some simple ways to raise your vibration to help connect with your soul.

172. Journal about what helps you feel connected

This might seem like a no-brainer, but many people haven't given themselves time to ponder what helps them feel good and connected to their souls. Use the space below to journal. Fill in the blank: When I feel connected _____.

....

....

....

....

....

....

....

....

....

....

....

....

....

....

....

....

....

....

....

173. Go out in nature

Nature is an instant soul-nourisher. Take five minutes and go outside. With deep breaths, pay attention to the trees, grass, flowers, water—anything that is part of nature. Use the space below to write about the one that inspired you the most and why.

....

....

....

....

....

....

....

....

....

....

....

....

....

....

....

....

....

....

174. Listen to your favorite music

There was a time in my life when I realized I hadn't listened to music in a long time. Music is an instant vibe-shifter. Take a moment to pull up your favorite song on YouTube today and listen.

Use the space below to write about how music makes you feel.

....

....

....

....

....

....

....

....

....

....

....

....

....

....

....

....

....

....

....

175. Create a playlist of your favorite upbeat songs

Take some time to create a playlist of your favorite songs that help move you into action. Shoot for an hour-long set of songs (about 18-20). You can push 'play' during a drive, housecleaning, or a workout.

Use the space below to get your list started.

....

....

....

....

....

....

....

....

....

....

....

....

....

....

....

....

....

....

176. Call someone you love and tell them

Simple but profound. Give someone a call today and tell them you love them.

Use the space below to journal about how it made you feel to think about doing this or how person's reaction made you feel.

....
....
....
....
....
....
....
....
....
....
....
....
....
....
....
....
....
....
....
....
....

177. Reach out to someone from your community who lives alone

Do you have a neighbor who lives alone? How about slipping a handwritten note in their mailbox today? Or maybe bringing them a small home-baked gift?

Use the space below to write about the feelings you have about this.

....

....

....

....

....

....

....

....

....

....

....

....

....

....

....

....

....

....

178. Watch a comedy show

Laughter is such wonderful medicine and an instant vibe-shifter. Choose one and watch!

Use the space below to write about laughter.

....

....

....

....

....

....

....

....

....

....

....

....

....

....

....

....

....

....

....

....

179. Write a post on your favorite social media platform that says, "Make me laugh."

See what comments you get. How long has it been since you spit out your milk because someone made you laugh like that?

Use the space below to write about what happens in your body when you laugh.

....

....

....

....

....

....

....

....

....

....

....

....

....

....

....

....

....

....

180. Inspire yourself; write yourself a list of why you're awesome

Gratitude lists are awesome, but have you ever done one for and about yourself? What makes you awesome? What are you grateful for about yourself? Use the space below to write out at least ten things or more.

....

....

....

....

....

....

....

....

....

....

....

....

....

....

....

....

....

....

....

....

181. Attend a community service event

Many local churches and community centers hold events. Check out a local online calendar and plan to help at an event.

Use the space below to journal about the experience.

....

....

....

....

....

....

....

....

....

....

....

....

....

....

....

....

....

....

....

182. Attend a lecture

Find a talk, book signing, or other lecture near you and plan to attend. Learning something new automatically shifts your vibe, not to mention the possibility of meeting someone who becomes a lifelong friend.

Use the space below to journal about how this idea makes you feel and then afterward, about the experience itself.

....

....

....

....

....

....

....

....

....

....

....

....

....

....

....

....

....

....

....

183. Make a list of everything you love

People, places, experiences, feelings, objects—list them all.
Use the space below.

....

....

....

....

....

....

....

....

....

....

....

....

....

....

....

....

....

....

....

....

....

....

184. Say aloud, "Everything is always working out for me."

Affirmations are an interesting activity with palpable results. How does it feel to say them out loud? Use the space below to write about that. Alternatively, you can also form a question from the statement: Why is everything always working out for me? Dr. Noah St. John calls these "afformations," and talks about why the questions work differently than statements.

....

....

....

....

....

....

....

....

....

....

....

....

....

....

....

....

....

185. Make a list of everything you have

Objects, friends, beliefs, knowledge, degrees, experiences, family—what are the things in your life that you already have?

Use the space below to list them and how it makes you feel to make that list.

....

....

....

....

....

....

....

....

....

....

....

....

....

....

....

....

....

....

....

186. Strike up a conversation about "The Universe" with someone you don't know

They say religion is not a topic to discuss with strangers, but this is different. Try starting a conversation with the term "The Universe" or "Higher power" and see what happens.

Use the space below to write about it.

....

....

....

....

....

....

....

....

....

....

....

....

....

....

....

....

....

....

....

187. Do some gardening or weeding

This activity is good for the soul in so many ways. Notice the sensations of the dirt, your gloves, the weather, and your deep breath. Use the space below to write about the experience.

....

....

....

....

....

....

....

....

....

....

....

....

....

....

....

....

....

....

....

188. Say out loud to yourself, "I feel deeply connected to my inner being."

This is an affirmation I love because connection is an instant energy shifter. You can also turn this into a question: Why do I always feel so deeply connected to my inner being?" Use the space below to write about connection.

....

....

....

....

....

....

....

....

....

....

....

....

....

....

....

....

....

....

....

....

189. Draw a picture of a tree from your yard

Creating any art will help you connect to your soul. If you don't consider yourself an artist, detach from that thought and see what happens.

Use the space below to sketch it, and then write about the experience.

....

....

....

....

....

....

....

....

....

....

....

....

....

....

....

....

....

....

....

190. Download the Night Sky App and find a constellation

There's nothing like the stars to help you feel wonder.

Use the space below to write about the stars and constellations you found.

....
....
....
....
....
....
....
....
....
....
....
....
....
....
....
....
....
....
....
....
....

191. Visit a music store and play with the instruments

I'm lost in the store for hours every time I do this. Whether you're a musician or not, playing with the instruments is fun and can shift your energy. If you have an instrument at home, play for a few minutes, and then use the space below to write about music.

....

....

....

....

....

....

....

....

....

....

....

....

....

....

....

....

....

....

192. Take a music lesson

Try a 30-minute music lesson, or search for one on YouTube and watch and enjoy.

Use the space below to write about the experience.

....

....

....

....

....

....

....

....

....

....

....

....

....

....

....

....

....

....

....

....

....

....

193. Say out loud to yourself, "I'm so happy and grateful to be alive."

If you're not quite matching this vibe today, you can try: "I'm alive," plain and simple. Take a deep breath and acknowledge what it feels like to be alive.

Use the space here to write about that.

....

....

....

....

....

....

....

....

....

....

....

....

....

....

....

....

....

....

....

....

194. Paint a rock

Any art is great for the soul, and painting rocks has to be one of the easiest ways to pull the artist out of you if you don't consider yourself one. Find a great rock in your neighborhood and a few paints. And you can even look up "Painted rocks" on Google to get some inspiration.

Use the space below to write about art, rocks, or whatever comes.

....
....
....
....
....
....
....
....
....
....
....
....
....
....
....
....
....
....
....

195. Drive to the mountains

A drive anywhere will do, but if you have a nearby mountain, take a drive and park at one of those scenic overlooks to take in the view, breathe, and ponder life.

Use the space below to write about the experience.

....

....

....

....

....

....

....

....

....

....

....

....

....

....

....

....

....

....

....

....

196. Write a love letter to your soulmate (or ideal soulmate)

Letters are amazing ways to connect in all different ways.

Use the space here to write a letter to your soulmate or ideal soulmate.

....

....

....

....

....

....

....

....

....

....

....

....

....

....

....

....

....

....

....

....

197. Look in the mirror and say, "I love you."

Were you able to look into your own eyes? What did you notice when you said the words out loud? Use the space below to write about it.

....

....

....

....

....

....

....

....

....

....

....

....

....

....

....

....

....

....

....

198. Make and send a handmade card

You'll find card stock paper at the art store. Grab a few markers, pens, or paint and create a handmade card. Choose someone to send it to with a personal note.

Use the space below to write about it.

....

....

....

....

....

....

....

....

....

....

....

....

....

....

....

....

....

....

....

....

199. Blow bubbles

Find some bubbles at the dollar store and spend five minutes blowing bubbles. Use the space below to write about how they looked and how you felt doing it.

....
....
....
....
....
....
....
....
....
....
....
....
....
....
....
....
....
....
....
....

200. Attend an open mic night near you

There are in-person and online versions of these events. Find one to attend, whether you plan on being a part of the show or not. Use the space below to write about it.

....
....
....
....
....
....
....
....
....
....
....
....
....
....
....
....
....
....
....
....
....
....

201. Think and write about the meaning of life

Use the space below to write about this topic. Try setting a timer for five minutes and write as fast as you can without censoring yourself.

....

....

....

....

....

....

....

....

....

....

....

....

....

....

....

....

....

....

....

....

202. Ask yourself, "What else is possible?"

Big questions will instantly shift your energy. This is one of my favorites.

Use the space below to write about what came up for you with this question.

....

....

....

....

....

....

....

....

....

....

....

....

....

....

....

....

....

....

....

....

....

203. Say out loud to yourself, "I'm whole and complete."

You aren't broken. There's nothing to fix. 'I am whole and complete' is a true statement. Say it out loud, and then write about this topic below.

....

....

....

....

....

....

....

....

....

....

....

....

....

....

....

....

....

....

....

....

204. Make a new recipe

Take out one of your favorite recipes and add a new ingredient that makes it your own new recipe. Use the space below to create it.

....

....

....

....

....

....

....

....

....

....

....

....

....

....

....

....

....

....

....

205. Search for "Zen Habits" on Amazon or Google and spend five minutes reading about this topic.

Use the space below to record your thoughts.

....

....

....

....

....

....

....

....

....

....

....

....

....

....

....

....

....

....

....

....

....

....

....

206. Go to YouTube and search for Nina Conti and listen to one of her shows

Nina is a brilliant puppeteer and comedian. Use the space below to write about how it made you feel to watch the puppets.

....

....

....

....

....

....

....

....

....

....

....

....

....

....

....

....

....

....

....

....

....

207. Offer to help someone

Whether it's a social post, a neighbor, a family member, friend, or stranger, offer to help someone today. Use the space below to write about the experience.

....

....

....

....

....

....

....

....

....

....

....

....

....

....

....

....

....

....

....

....

....

208. Say out loud to yourself, "I'm a powerful communicator and guide."

Or use the question instead: Why am I such a powerful communicator and guide?"

Use the space below to write about this.

....
....
....
....
....
....
....
....
....
....
....
....
....
....
....
....
....
....
....
....
....

209. Search for Dakota Earth Cloud Walker on YouTube and listen to a free meditation

Use the space here to write about anything that came up during your experience.

....

....

....

....

....

....

....

....

....

....

....

....

....

....

....

....

....

....

....

....

210. Go to www.the10minutemind.com and listen to a free sample.

Use the space below to write about what came up.

....

....

....

....

....

....

....

....

....

....

....

....

....

....

....

....

....

....

....

....

....

....

211. Go slower with everything

Today, try taking one normal task you usually complete and slow way down. Notice everything about each step of the activity. What's it feel like to slow way down?

Use the space here to write about how that felt.

....
....
....
....
....
....
....
....
....
....
....
....
....
....
....
....
....
....
....

212. Make a chalk drawing on the sidewalk or walkway

You can find chalk at the dollar store or online. Enjoy the process of thinking about what you want to draw, the feel of the chalk, and the connection with the surface you're drawing on as your canvas. Use the space below to write about it afterward.

....

....

....

....

....

....

....

....

....

....

....

....

....

....

....

....

....

....

....

....

213. Get a tarot card reading

You can find a friend who does this or pull a card for yourself today. Don't own a tarot card deck? Explore tarot.com

Use the space below to write about anything that came up.

....
....
....
....
....
....
....
....
....
....
....
....
....
....
....
....
....
....
....
....

214. Write a letter to your higher self asking for what you want

We often have an idea about what we want but forget to ask. Use the space below to write a letter that begins with the words, "Thank you so much for. . . " and write as if you've already received it and how you're feeling.

....

....

....

....

....

....

....

....

....

....

....

....

....

....

....

....

....

....

....

....

....

215. Take an online class on soul-nourishing

You'd be amazed at what you find when you Google "Classes about soul nourishing." Do some reading, take a class, or listen to a video. Use the space below to record your takeaways.

....

....

....

....

....

....

....

....

....

....

....

....

....

....

....

....

....

....

....

....

216. Set a timer for five minutes and write as fast as you can without censoring yourself

My soul was meant for _____.

Use the space below to write.

....

....

....

....

....

....

....

....

....

....

....

....

....

....

....

....

....

....

....

....

217. Say out loud to yourself, "I'm okay."

When you say this, depending on how you're feeling, you'll notice a response in your body.

Use the space below to write about those sensations.

....

....

....

....

....

....

....

....

....

....

....

....

....

....

....

....

....

....

....

....

218. Say aloud, "I have everything I need within me."

Spend five minutes meditating on this statement. Get quiet and listen to what comes. Use the space below to note down anything you noticed.

....

....

....

....

....

....

....

....

....

....

....

....

....

....

....

....

....

....

....

....

....

219. Believe in yourself

What is something you want to do? Are you your best cheerleader? Ask yourself, "Do I believe I can do this?" And then, use the space below to write about this.

....

....

....

....

....

....

....

....

....

....

....

....

....

....

....

....

....

....

....

....

220. Say a prayer out loud

Pay particular attention to how you word your prayer. Instead of using language about what you're worried about, try wording the prayer as a "thank you" for what will be delivered.

Use the space below to write your prayer.

....

....

....

....

....

....

....

....

....

....

....

....

....

....

....

....

....

....

....

221. Set a timer for five minutes and write as fast as you can without censoring yourself

When I connect to my intuition _____.

Use the space below to write.

....

....

....

....

....

....

....

....

....

....

....

....

....

....

....

....

....

....

....

....

....

222. Sing

Anything will do. Happy birthday works. If you have to go for a drive so nobody hears you, then do it. Sing bold and loud. Notice the way the vibration feels inside.

Use the space below to write about it.

....

....

....

....

....

....

....

....

....

....

....

....

....

....

....

....

....

....

....

....

223. Read *A New Earth*, by Eckhart Tolle

This book was the start of my next-level awareness journey. Read an excerpt today and use the space below to write about any takeaways.

....

....

....

....

....

....

....

....

....

....

....

....

....

....

....

....

....

....

....

224. Look up your spirit animal (notice what animals show up in your world)

I love the book *Spirit Animal Medicine* by Dr. Stephen Farmer. You can look them up on Google too. Read a little bit, then use the space below to write about your takeaways.

....
....
....
....
....
....
....
....
....
....
....
....
....
....
....
....
....
....
....
....
....
....

225. Read *Being Peace* by Thich Nhat Hanh

Read one chapter or an excerpt from the internet and then use the space below to write your reflections on the topic.

....
....
....
....
....
....
....
....
....
....
....
....
....
....
....
....
....
....
....
....
....
....

226. Lie on your back and watch the clouds

I remember doing this as a kid. It's been a while. Find a great place to lie down and gaze at the cloudy sky. What do you see?

Use the space below to write about the experience.

....

....

....

....

....

....

....

....

....

....

....

....

....

....

....

....

....

....

....

....

227. Just let go of your thoughts for five minutes

This is a simple meditation challenge. Breathe and clear your mind. Focus on the sensation of your breath. Use the space below to write about anything that came to you.

....

....

....

....

....

....

....

....

....

....

....

....

....

....

....

....

....

....

....

....

....

....

228. Say no to that extra invitation

We sometimes tend to say yes when we mean no. If you have FOMO (fear of missing out) and end up over-scheduling yourself, this time, say no without any explanation. Use the space below to write about how that felt.

....

....

....

....

....

....

....

....

....

....

....

....

....

....

....

....

....

....

....

....

229. Look at old pictures from a positive time in your life

Take a few minutes and pull out some old pictures you love. Notice how they make you feel, and use the space below to journal about that time in your life.

....

....

....

....

....

....

....

....

....

....

....

....

....

....

....

....

....

....

....

....

230. Avoid all media (TV, radio, social media) for one day

Use the space below to write about how that went.

....
....
....
....
....
....
....
....
....
....
....
....
....
....
....
....
....
....
....
....
....
....
....

231. Stand up for someone who can't

Notice something unfair? Speak up for someone who is not able to. Use the space below to write about how this felt for you, whether you spoke up or were unable to.

....
....
....
....
....
....
....
....
....
....
....
....
....
....
....
....
....
....
....
....
....
....

232. Appreciate something beautiful

What is beautiful to you? Use the space below to write about it and why it's beautiful.

....
....
....
....
....
....
....
....
....
....
....
....
....
....
....
....
....
....
....
....
....
....
....

233. Listen to ancient chanting from Buddhist and Gregorian monks

You can search for this on YouTube and find one that interests you. Use the space below to write about how this made you feel and anything that came up.

....

....

....

....

....

....

....

....

....

....

....

....

....

....

....

....

....

....

....

....

234. Practice Ho'oponopono

"I'm sorry. Please forgive me. Thank you. I love you."
Those are the four phrases of Ho'oponopono. Research this
ancient Hawaiian technique a little, try saying the phrases,
and then use this space to write about any takeaways.

....
....
....
....
....
....
....
....
....
....
....
....
....
....
....
....
....
....
....
....
....
....

235. Say out loud to yourself, "New friends appear in my life in unexpected ways."

You're never too old for a new friend. Notice how it feels to say this out loud and then use the space below to write about this.

....

....

....

....

....

....

....

....

....

....

....

....

....

....

....

....

....

....

....

....

....

....

236. Say out loud to yourself, "My intuition is strong."

Soul connection is partly about connecting with your intuitive power. How does it feel to say this out loud? What does intuition mean to you? Use the space here to write about it.

....

....

....

....

....

....

....

....

....

....

....

....

....

....

....

....

....

....

....

....

....

PART FOUR

SHIFTING TO GOOD VIBES FROM ANGER OR RAGE

I added these in because sometimes the vibe you're carrying feels a little more intense, and it's extremely therapeutic to give yourself permission to acknowledge those feelings and then consciously shift them.

For this section, the feeling comes first. Then use the prompts to honor that feeling and shift it when you're ready.

Any of the activities in this section can be done by visualizing them if you can't complete them safely. And ultimately, if anger or rage is a problem, talk to a professional who deals with this topic and get help!

237. Drive in the car and sing along with loud music playing

Choose your music depending on your mood. What would be most therapeutic for you? Use the space below to write about the experience or any leftover sensations.

....

....

....

....

....

....

....

....

....

....

....

....

....

....

....

....

....

....

....

....

238. Journal everything you feel without censoring yourself

Use the space below.

....

....

....

....

....

....

....

....

....

....

....

....

....

....

....

....

....

....

....

....

....

239. Scream as loud and long as you need to into a pillow

Use the space below to write about any of the sensations or what came up.

....

....

....

....

....

....

....

....

....

....

....

....

....

....

....

....

....

....

....

....

....

240. Punch a pillow until you're tired

You can start with a light punch and build up to what feels good. Use the space below to write about what came up.

....

....

....

....

....

....

....

....

....

....

....

....

....

....

....

....

....

....

....

....

....

241. Write a letter to the person or situation you're angry with and then burn it

Don't censor yourself. Use the space below to write.

....
....
....
....
....
....
....
....
....
....
....
....
....
....
....
....
....
....
....
....
....
....
....

242. Talk to anyone you trust

Sometimes reaching out is best in times of intense emotion. Can you chat with a friend for five minutes? Let them know you're giving yourself a time limit to talk about your feelings. Then, come back and use the space below to write about it.

....

....

....

....

....

....

....

....

....

....

....

....

....

....

....

....

....

....

....

....

243. Take a boxing class online or in-person

Use the space below to write about the experience.

....

....

....

....

....

....

....

....

....

....

....

....

....

....

....

....

....

....

....

....

....

....

....

....

244. Sign up for a martial arts class

What did you learn? Use the space below to write about it.

....

....

....

....

....

....

....

....

....

....

....

....

....

....

....

....

....

....

....

....

....

....

245. Kick or punch a kicking bag until you're tired

If you don't have access to a professional bag, try a sofa pillow. Do this with good shoes on if you're kicking! Use the space below to write about anything that came up.

....

....

....

....

....

....

....

....

....

....

....

....

....

....

....

....

....

....

....

....

246. Break old dishes

You'll have to find a safe space where the clean-up is easy and possible. I've seen special events for this activity online. Wear glasses or your ski goggles, and go for it.

Use the space here to write about what came up for you.

....

....

....

....

....

....

....

....

....

....

....

....

....

....

....

....

....

....

....

....

247. Stomp your feet

Remember stomping your feet on the bleachers at school during a game? Same idea. Make sure you have good shoes on. Feel free to make a noise while you stomp.

Use the space below to write about what came up for you.

....
....
....
....
....
....
....
....
....
....
....
....
....
....
....
....
....
....
....
....
....

248. Give yourself permission to be angry

Use the space below to write yourself a permission slip.

....

....

....

....

....

....

....

....

....

....

....

....

....

....

....

....

....

....

....

....

....

....

....

....

249. Talk to a therapist

I mentioned this at the beginning of this section, but talking to a professional who has a new perspective and can share tools for releasing anger is powerful. Give it a try.

Use the space below to write about this. Do you have feelings about talking to someone?

....

....

....

....

....

....

....

....

....

....

....

....

....

....

....

....

....

....

250. Attend a group support session

Many group therapy and coaching programs offer assistance when you're feeling this kind of intense emotion. Spend a few minutes researching this today. See what you find.

Use the space to write about what comes up. Reach out to the organization if appropriate.

....

....

....

....

....

....

....

....

....

....

....

....

....

....

....

....

....

....

....

251. Listen to one of Tara Brach's meditations on anger

https://www.tarabrach.com/part-1-awakening-anger/

Use the space below to write about any takeaways.

....

....

....

....

....

....

....

....

....

....

....

....

....

....

....

....

....

....

....

....

....

....

....

252. Recognize worst-case scenario thinking and flip the switch to something better

When do you automatically cycle to worst-case thinking?

Use the space below to flip your switch and write about what else is possible.

....

....

....

....

....

....

....

....

....

....

....

....

....

....

....

....

....

....

....

....

253. Read about anger

Spend a moment researching the topic to see what you find. Read about it for five minutes, and then use the space below to record any takeaways.

....

....

....

....

....

....

....

....

....

....

....

....

....

....

....

....

....

....

....

....

254. Look up "Meditation for Anger" on YouTube and listen to one

Use the space below to record any takeaways.

....

....

....

....

....

....

....

....

....

....

....

....

....

....

....

....

....

....

....

....

....

255. Go to www.Listeningtosmile.com and listen to a free track

Use the space below to write about what you felt.

....

....

....

....

....

....

....

....

....

....

....

....

....

....

....

....

....

....

....

....

....

....

....

....

256. Set a timer for five minutes and write as fast as you can without censoring yourself

All this anger feels like _____.

Use the space below to write.

....
....
....
....
....
....
....
....
....
....
....
....
....
....
....
....
....
....
....
....
....

257. Look up Abraham Hicks on YouTube and search for "Rage is Okay, Just Don't Get Stuck."

Use the space below to write after you listen.

....
....
....
....
....
....
....
....
....
....
....
....
....
....
....
....
....
....
....
....
....
....
....
....

258. Go for a brisk walk or run

Movement is therapeutic when feelings are intense. Use the space below to write about how you felt afterward.

....
....
....
....
....
....
....
....
....
....
....
....
....
....
....
....
....
....
....
....
....
....

259. Go to the batting cage or driving range

These are great ways to deal with anger therapeutically. Use the space below to write about anything that came up.

....

....

....

....

....

....

....

....

....

....

....

....

....

....

....

....

....

....

....

....

....

....

....

PART FIVE

OTHER KINDS
OF GOOD VIBES

Here's another section with more great vibe-shifting prompts.

260. Wash your car to your favorite music

I love washing my car. The trick here is not to rush and enjoy the experience. Enjoy the process, whether in your driveway or at the car wash. Use the space here to write about what you noticed.

....
....
....
....
....
....
....
....
....
....
....
....
....
....
....
....
....
....
....
....
....

261. Pet your dog or cat

Spend five minutes petting your pet. Use the space below to write about what you noticed.

....

....

....

....

....

....

....

....

....

....

....

....

....

....

....

....

....

....

....

....

....

262. Declutter a small corner of your home/purse/drawer

You can eventually Feng Shui your whole house, but today, pick a small corner, clear it out, throw away the junk, and clean the space. Use the space below to write about how it made you feel.

....

....

....

....

....

....

....

....

....

....

....

....

....

....

....

....

....

....

....

....

263. Light an awesome-smelling candle or incense

Candles, incense, or smudge can be great energy shifters. Try one. Use the space here to write about anything you felt.

....

....

....

....

....

....

....

....

....

....

....

....

....

....

....

....

....

....

....

....

....

264. Go to the coffee shop

Take a trip for a cuppa Joe. Notice everything about the outing. Use the space here to describe the people, shop, coffee, and what you saw, smelled, tasted, or heard.

....
....
....
....
....
....
....
....
....
....
....
....
....
....
....
....
....
....
....
....
....
....
....

265. Color in a coloring book

You can find great coloring pages online that you can print for free. Spend five minutes coloring, and then use the space below to write about how you felt.

....

....

....

....

....

....

....

....

....

....

....

....

....

....

....

....

....

....

....

....

....

266. Doodle

Doodling is therapeutic. Don't attach to the outcome. Just put a pencil or pen on paper and go for it. Spend five minutes doodling in the space below and then write about how that felt.

....

....

....

....

....

....

....

....

....

....

....

....

....

....

....

....

....

....

....

....

267. Write a poem

What is something you love to do ?Write a poem that helps you smell, taste, touch, hear, and feel that. Use the space below.

....

....

....

....

....

....

....

....

....

....

....

....

....

....

....

....

....

....

....

....

268. Read a poem

Look up one of your favorite poets online and read a poem out loud. Use the space below to record your favorite line and write about why it was your favorite.

....

....

....

....

....

....

....

....

....

....

....

....

....

....

....

....

....

....

....

....

....

269. Read one page of an inspiring book

Pick any book you have, want, or can borrow and read one page. Use the space below to write about your takeaway.

....

....

....

....

....

....

....

....

....

....

....

....

....

....

....

....

....

....

....

....

....

270. Make a healthy meal

Look up a recipe for something healthy you've wanted to try and make it! Notice what you love about the way it tastes. Use the space below to write about it.

....

....

....

....

....

....

....

....

....

....

....

....

....

....

....

....

....

....

....

....

....

271. Smudge your living space

You can use sage, Palo Santo, or homemade herbs. You'll find recipes online or check your local health food store. Look up the proper technique for smudging online and clear a room in your home by smudging. Use the space below to write about the experience.

....

....

....

....

....

....

....

....

....

....

....

....

....

....

....

....

....

....

....

....

272. Bask in the full moon

Look up the date of the next full moon and make a date with yourself for a meditation session. Focus on basking in the light and energy for at least five minutes. Come back and write about anything that came to you.

....

....

....

....

....

....

....

....

....

....

....

....

....

....

....

....

....

....

....

273. Clean your kitchen countertops

Clean spaces are important for your energy and vibe, especially those you work, cook, or create on. Use a homemade cleaner (white vinegar and water work well) and clean one of your countertops. Use the space below to write about how that felt.

....

....

....

....

....

....

....

....

....

....

....

....

....

....

....

....

....

....

....

274. Clean anything

Choose something to clean. Areas you spend the most time in are great choices. Dust, clear, clean, or otherwise make that area sparkle. Use the space below to write about how cleaning felt to you.

....

....

....

....

....

....

....

....

....

....

....

....

....

....

....

....

....

....

....

....

....

....

....

275. Rearrange the furniture

Is there an area of your home that feels tight, heavy, or doesn't make you feel good? How can you rearrange the room to lighten up the energy? Play with the ideas and use the space below to plan.

....

....

....

....

....

....

....

....

....

....

....

....

....

....

....

....

....

....

276. Plan a Good Vibes party

Invite one or more than one person or your cat; it doesn't matter. Use the space below to plan your good vibes party. What does that look like?

....
....
....
....
....
....
....
....
....
....
....
....
....
....
....
....
....
....
....
....
....
....

277. Attend a book club meeting

You'll find the awesome Brave Healer Book Club on Facebook here:

https://www.facebook.com/groups/143744423674578
Or you can research events online. Use the space below to record the options and your plan.

....

....

....

....

....

....

....

....

....

....

....

....

....

....

....

....

....

....

278. Diffuse an essential oil

Essential oils can be fantastic vibe shifters. Do a little research on DoTerra.com or YoungLiving.com (my two faves) and decide which one you'd like to try. Use the space below to write about what you noticed.

....
....
....
....
....
....
....
....
....
....
....
....
....
....
....
....
....
....
....
....
....

279. Bring a neighbor a casserole

Know a neighbor who has been going through a tough time? What if you just brought them a casserole for the heck of it, whether they've had a tough time or not? Any small, medium, or large treat will do. It's more about the thought and act. Use the space below to write about what you felt.

....

....

....

....

....

....

....

....

....

....

....

....

....

....

....

....

....

....

....

280. Write a thank you note to someone

You can write a note, email, or text someone right now! Who do you want to thank? Use the space below to craft the note.

....

....

....

....

....

....

....

....

....

....

....

....

....

....

....

....

....

....

....

....

....

281. Buy a crystal and Google how to use it

Crystals have magical energy, and there are many types used for many different things. You can research them and find out more. Do you have any around the house? Try looking it up and use the space below to write any information you want to remember.

....
....
....
....
....
....
....
....
....
....
....
....
....
....
....
....
....
....
....
....

282. Photograph five different kinds of flowers

I love this activity. You can use your phone or a camera to go on a nature expedition for five awesome photos. It can be flowers, trees, or anything that catches the eye.

Use the space below to write about each of the five photos.

....

....

....

....

....

....

....

....

....

....

....

....

....

....

....

....

....

....

....

....

283. Go somewhere dark and watch for shooting stars

Do you know a location away from the city lights where you can gaze at the night sky and watch for shooting stars? Take five minutes on a warm evening and watch the sky. Use the space below to write about the experience.

....

....

....

....

....

....

....

....

....

....

....

....

....

....

....

....

....

....

....

....

284. Unsubscribe from all email newsletters you never read

You know the ones! Spend five to fifteen minutes unsubscribing. This is a digital decluttering activity. Yes, you can Feng Shui your inbox! Use the space below to write about any takeaways or what you noticed.

....

....

....

....

....

....

....

....

....

....

....

....

....

....

....

....

....

....

....

....

285. Turn off the television and meditate

The next time you catch yourself zoning out on TV, turn it off and meditate instead. Close your eyes and focus on your breath for ten minutes.

Use the space below to record any takeaways.

....
....
....
....
....
....
....
....
....
....
....
....
....
....
....
....
....
....
....
....

286. Text someone, "I love you."

Use the space below to write about love.

....

....

....

....

....

....

....

....

....

....

....

....

....

....

....

....

....

....

....

....

....

....

....

287. Throw out any clothing you haven't worn in a year

If it's been through four seasons and hasn't moved from your closet or drawers, it's time to go. Decluttering the belongings you don't use makes room for new energy to flow to you. Use the space below to plan your next decluttering journey.

....

....

....

....

....

....

....

....

....

....

....

....

....

....

....

....

....

....

288. Donate some time or money to your favorite charity

Use the space below to list a few of your favorite organizations and why. Plan to donate either money or time.

....
....
....
....
....
....
....
....
....
....
....
....
....
....
....
....
....
....
....
....
....

289. Send a small gift to someone as a surprise

Even a card will do. Sometimes I'll slip feathers, bookmarks, or other small gifts into the card as an extra special surprise. Use the space below to write about gifts. How does giving and receiving feel to you?

....

....

....

....

....

....

....

....

....

....

....

....

....

....

....

....

....

....

....

290. Join a group about your favorite hobby

Research LinkedIn, Facebook, or Meetup groups and find one you want to join. Attend a meeting or event and see how it goes. Use the space below to record any thoughts about your hobby. Why do you love it? When did you start it?

....
....
....
....
....
....
....
....
....
....
....
....
....
....
....
....
....
....
....
....
....

291. See how slowly you can eat your next meal

Mindful eating will shift the energy immediately. See how it goes. Chew each bite at least 25 times. How does that feel? Use the space here to write about it.

....

....

....

....

....

....

....

....

....

....

....

....

....

....

....

....

....

....

....

....

292. Put your phone away for half a day

Choose a day that doesn't add stress to your schedule and protect the commitment. Notice how it makes you feel. You can warn your VIP list you're doing it first if that helps. Use the space below to write about today's technology and how it makes you feel to be addicted to that instant access to people.

....

....

....

....

....

....

....

....

....

....

....

....

....

....

....

....

....

....

....

....

293. Open a window and feel the breeze

Spend five minutes noticing what you feel. Use the space below to write about it.

....

....

....

....

....

....

....

....

....

....

....

....

....

....

....

....

....

....

....

....

....

....

294. Watch the sunrise or sunset

Linger in the gaze until the light is fully transformed. Use the space to write about what inspired you the most.

....
....
....
....
....
....
....
....
....
....
....
....
....
....
....
....
....
....
....
....
....
....
....

295. Sit at the ocean and watch the waves

If you don't have access to the ocean, a river, stream, or even a pond will do! Spend at least five minutes meditating on what you notice. Use the space below to write about what you feel.

....

....

....

....

....

....

....

....

....

....

....

....

....

....

....

....

....

....

....

296. Write a letter to your kids (or any kid) about life lessons you've learned

What would you want the younger generation to know? What's the biggest life lesson you'd like to share? Write a letter in the space below.

....

....

....

....

....

....

....

....

....

....

....

....

....

....

....

....

....

....

....

....

....

....

....

297. Write a bucket list

Anything goes here. It could be places you want to visit or experiences you want to have. Use the space below to list them.

....
....
....
....
....
....
....
....
....
....
....
....
....
....
....
....
....
....
....
....
....

298. Walk in your neighborhood with the goal of talking to someone

If you feel safe in your neighborhood, take a stroll to say hello and start a conversation with someone. What do you notice about the interaction? Use the space here to write about it.

....

....

....

....

....

....

....

....

....

....

....

....

....

....

....

....

....

....

....

....

299. Strike up a conversation with the grocery store clerk about something you notice about them

Challenge yourself next time you're at the checkout counter. What do you notice about the clerk you can compliment or comment on that would make them smile? Use the space below to write about the experience.

....

....

....

....

....

....

....

....

....

....

....

....

....

....

....

....

....

....

....

....

300. Complement someone

Anyone. In any way. Notice and write.

....
....
....
....
....
....
....
....
....
....
....
....
....
....
....
....
....
....
....
....
....
....
....

301. Connect with an animal

Walk the dog, a neighbor's dog, or volunteer at the rescue near you. You could visit a local petting zoo, the actual zoo, or a nearby horse farm. Notice everything you can about the experience. Write about it here.

....

....

....

....

....

....

....

....

....

....

....

....

....

....

....

....

....

....

....

....

302. Offer to house or pet sit

Does someone you know travel a lot and need help? Make a genuine offer to pet or house sit. It's just the offer experience we're after here, whether they take you up on it or not. Use the space below to write about offering help and how it feels when someone accepts or declines.

....
....
....
....
....
....
....
....
....
....
....
....
....
....
....
....
....
....
....
....

303. Attend a fundraiser

What organizations do you stand behind? What events are they holding soon? Research one and plan to attend online or in-person. Use the space here to write about what that organization means to you.

....

....

....

....

....

....

....

....

....

....

....

....

....

....

....

....

....

....

....

....

....

304. Google "Parks near me" and choose one to visit

Make a plan to visit a park. You can walk, sit, or frolic; it's up to you. What do you notice? Write about it here.

....
....
....
....
....
....
....
....
....
....
....
....
....
....
....
....
....
....
....
....
....
....
....

305. Test drive your dream car

You have to be 18 for this one. Have fun with it, even if you ask the salesperson to drive. What is your dream car? Write about it here.

....

....

....

....

....

....

....

....

....

....

....

....

....

....

....

....

....

....

....

....

....

306. Take a moment for self-care

Do one self-care activity for 30 minutes today. Whatever feels the most decadent and nourishing. Use the space here to journal about what you felt.

....

....

....

....

....

....

....

....

....

....

....

....

....

....

....

....

....

....

....

....

....

307. Have lunch (or a phone call) with a good friend

Use the space here to list your best friends, the ones you trust and love to talk to, who always make you feel like a better person. Call one of them!

....

....

....

....

....

....

....

....

....

....

....

....

....

....

....

....

....

....

....

....

....

308. Make a collage in your journal with a "love" or "gratitude theme

An easy way to do this is by cutting up magazines and using the pictures or words. Your journal page becomes a small vision board. You can use the space here to journal about the theme of your journal page or what came up for you. You can even do the collage right here on this page.

....

....

....

....

....

....

....

....

....

....

....

....

....

....

....

....

....

....

....

309. Watch a dog or cat video on YouTube or Instagram

The dog videos on @dachshund_dogys are my fave. Write about your favorite one and why.

....
....
....
....
....
....
....
....
....
....
....
....
....
....
....
....
....
....
....
....
....
....

310. Knit, crochet, or needlepoint

If you've never tried it, look it up on YouTube to see which one you'd like to try. You'll need a few basic supplies for this. If thread isn't your thing, find some photos of magnificent pieces of thread art and write about how they made you feel.

....
....
....
....
....
....
....
....
....
....
....
....
....
....
....
....
....
....
....
....
....

311. Take a day trip

What's a local-ish destination you can get to in an hour or so that you can make a day trip out of? Use the space here to list some of the places you want to visit and what you want to see when you get there. Journal as you go!

....

....

....

....

....

....

....

....

....

....

....

....

....

....

....

....

....

....

312. Have a bed picnic

Breakfast, lunch, or dinner in bed is awesome. Set out a big blanket or sheet over your normal comforter, so you don't drop food and stain your bedding. Add a towel and napkins for extra protection. Set up your favorite music or Netflix special and totally chill. Journal a little bit too.

....

....

....

....

....

....

....

....

....

....

....

....

....

....

....

....

....

....

....

313. Plan a vacation

You can even plan a staycation. This can be a one-day event or a 10-day Caribbean extravaganza. It's the planning I want you to focus on. Use the space below to see what comes up as you feel exactly what this vacation will look, smell, taste, sound, and feel like.

....

....

....

....

....

....

....

....

....

....

....

....

....

....

....

....

....

....

....

....

314. Donate blankets or old pet equipment to a local animal shelter

Gather your old stuff from Fido and bring it to your local shelter. Write about what you noticed.

....

....

....

....

....

....

....

....

....

....

....

....

....

....

....

....

....

....

....

....

....

....

....

315. Do a few Mad Libs

Remember those? Research this and find a good one to try. Write about your favorite line.

....
....
....
....
....
....
....
....
....
....
....
....
....
....
....
....
....
....
....
....
....
....

316. Practice calligraphy

You can look this up, take a class, or just play with a new pen. Try it! There is a strong hand-to-brain connection when you write. Practice on this page!

....

....

....

....

....

....

....

....

....

....

....

....

....

....

....

....

....

....

....

....

....

317. Clean your plants

Take a soft dust rag and gently dust your plant's leaves. Dust is an energy flow blocker. For a bonus, talk to your plants as you do this. Write about your ideas or what you notice. FYI: all my plants have names. Eddie Van Halen is my fave. He is my rock star plant.

....
....
....
....
....
....
....
....
....
....
....
....
....
....
....
....
....
....
....

318. Take your lunch outside

Today, take your meal outside and bask in the sunlight while you eat. Bring your journal and write about what you notice.

....

....

....

....

....

....

....

....

....

....

....

....

....

....

....

....

....

....

....

....

....

....

319. Create a special space in your yard to read

Can you create a sacred reading or relaxation space in your yard, patio, or porch? What could you do to create that space for yourself? Use the space here to make a plan.

....

....

....

....

....

....

....

....

....

....

....

....

....

....

....

....

....

....

....

....

....

320. Paint your front door in your favorite color

Mine is bright royal blue. Ever since I painted it, I've loved the energy. Your front door is a significant place in Feng Shui. It's a welcoming place. What kind of energy does your front door have? How does it make you feel to be at your home's entryway? If you can't paint, wash your front door with soap and water to clear the energy! Write about this below.

....

....

....

....

....

....

....

....

....

....

....

....

....

....

....

....

....

....

321. Say out loud to yourself, "Money comes to me easily."

This affirmation can trigger some old blocks. Notice what happens when you say it out loud. You can also use the question: Why does money come so easily to me? Write about money in the space below. How does having it, or not having enough, make you feel? Call out your own money beliefs and blocks here!

....

....

....

....

....

....

....

....

....

....

....

....

....

....

....

....

....

....

322. Groom your dog or cat

Spend time with a brush, comb, or damp washcloth and groom your pet. If you don't have a pet, do this for yourself with a hairbrush, comb, or another grooming device. What kind of pampering can you bestow upon your pet or yourself today? Write about how it felt.

....
....
....
....
....
....
....
....
....
....
....
....
....
....
....
....
....
....
....
....
....

323. Find a high-vibe accountability partner

When you're having trouble staying accountable to your life dreams or goals or making them in the first place, it's nice to have a partner who can help you. Choose someone you love and make an invitation to them. This is as much for them as it is for you. Use the space below to craft your invitation and write about how it's making you feel.

....

....

....

....

....

....

....

....

....

....

....

....

....

....

....

....

....

....

....

324. Send a letter to someone who has impacted your life in a positive way

Use the space below to write a letter to someone who helped you live an awesome life or impacted you in any positive way.

....

....

....

....

....

....

....

....

....

....

....

....

....

....

....

....

....

....

....

....

....

....

325. Put together a bag of coats to donate to your local shelter

If you have any old coats, scarves, hats, or gloves you don't wear anymore, consider gathering them and donating them to one of your local organizations. GoGreenDrop.com has a great system to make donating easy. Use this space to write about the abundance you feel and everything you're grateful for.

....

....

....

....

....

....

....

....

....

....

....

....

....

....

....

....

....

....

....

326. Clean everything from under your bed

The under-the-bed space can become cluttered and dusty. Clearing and cleaning that space can free up some stagnant energy in your bedroom. Time to break out the donation bag, especially if you haven't seen what's under there in over a year. Use the space below to write about letting go and how it feels.

....

....

....

....

....

....

....

....

....

....

....

....

....

....

....

....

....

....

....

327. Hang a wind chime

Ah, the energy-shifting power of a chime, especially fun on a windy day. Notice what you feel when you hear the sound and write about it. You can even find a small bell to try this with.

....

....

....

....

....

....

....

....

....

....

....

....

....

....

....

....

....

....

....

....

328. Set up a bird feeder

If you have the space to hang a bird feeder, try it. You can find inexpensive ones at the hardware store or online. Notice the birds that come and research them. Write about how the birds make you feel. If you don't have space for a feeder, try a little birdwatching at the park.

....

....

....

....

....

....

....

....

....

....

....

....

....

....

....

....

....

....

....

....

329. Plant some flowers

You can manage this in a big or small way. A garden or a windowsill pot are both options. You can plant flowers or herbs, whatever is easiest. Nature is an instant vibe-shifter. How can you bring some more nature into your immediate world? Write about the nature connection here. What does it mean to you?

....

....

....

....

....

....

....

....

....

....

....

....

....

....

....

....

....

....

330. Pick or buy some fresh flowers for your room

Flowers enhance the energy of the room and magnetize it. What colors or varieties are your favorites? List a few of your favorites and why in the space below.

....

....

....

....

....

....

....

....

....

....

....

....

....

....

....

....

....

....

....

....

....

....

331. Add a live plant to your living space

Plants are great for your home and help to detoxify it. One of the easiest plants to keep alive indoors is the Golden Pothos. Take a moment to choose a special place for your new addition, and use the space below to write about how it makes you feel to add a plant to your space. Are you going to name it?

....
....
....
....
....
....
....
....
....
....
....
....
....
....
....
....
....
....
....

332. Bake yourself a cake

You don't need an occasion. Take some time today and bake a cake for yourself. What flavor is your favorite? This cake is just for you. Take your time. Bake with love. And use the space below to write down your thoughts about baking for yourself. How is it different than baking for someone else?

....
....
....
....
....
....
....
....
....
....
....
....
....
....
....
....
....
....
....
....
....
....

333. Say "I love you" today

It could be to yourself or to someone you love. It could be to a pet or a plant. It's just about the vibration of love. When you say it, you are creating those vibes inside of yourself. Use the space below to write about how love feels inside you.

....

....

....

....

....

....

....

....

....

....

....

....

....

....

....

....

....

....

....

....

334. Find the lyrics to your favorite song and read them out loud

Song lyrics are interesting when read. Sometimes we miss them when we hear a song on the radio or played from our playlist. Words have power. Notice the words in the lyrics of your favorite song. How do they make you feel? What do you notice? What words resonate the most? Write about that in the space below.

....

....

....

....

....

....

....

....

....

....

....

....

....

....

....

....

....

....

335. Write a great review for a local business you frequent

This is a form of gratitude energy in action. Try writing a review on Yelp, Google, or on social media. Tag the business owner if you can, or email the review to them so they can use it on their online sites. What specific value did you receive? What result? How did their service make you feel or help you? Use the space below to craft your review.

....

....

....

....

....

....

....

....

....

....

....

....

....

....

....

....

....

....

....

336. Watch a happy movie

I love movies that leave me with a happy vibe. What's a movie you have on your list like this? You may have watched it before, or it may be new. Ask your friends for recommendations. List some of your favorite happy movies below. Choose one to watch. Journal below about the feeling.

....

....

....

....

....

....

....

....

....

....

....

....

....

....

....

....

....

....

....

337. Smile at someone

You can choose someone in your home or a stranger in a park, store, or on the street. Make this the best-ever smile with great eye contact. Let that linger for a moment. See what happens. Use the space below to write about how smiling made you feel.

....

....

....

....

....

....

....

....

....

....

....

....

....

....

....

....

....

....

....

....

....

338. Get a project done early

If you're working on something with a deadline, try completing it early and see how that feels. Use the space below to write about deadlines and how you are with them.

....

....

....

....

....

....

....

....

....

....

....

....

....

....

....

....

....

....

....

....

....

339. Put glow-in-the-dark stars on your ceiling

You can use stickers or plastic stars you can find online, or do anything with glitter or extra sparkle in any space you want. In general, add something eye-catching and energizing to your space to add some energy. Use the space below to write about spaces that help you feel excited and energized.

....

....

....

....

....

....

....

....

....

....

....

....

....

....

....

....

....

....

....

....

....

340. Go to the zoo

Do an outing to the zoo and journal everything about your favorite animal.

....
....
....
....
....
....
....
....
....
....
....
....
....
....
....
....
....
....
....
....
....
....
....

341. Stop hanging out with negative people

If someone in your life is consistently negative and you're feeling weighed down by that, let them know, or stop saying yes to spending time with them. Protect your good vibes. You come first. You can only live a high-vibe life when the people you spend time with practice high vibes and help you feel that way. Use the space below to journal about this topic. Is there someone making this challenging?

....

....

....

....

....

....

....

....

....

....

....

....

....

....

....

....

....

....

342. Shift gossip to praise

If you catch yourself gossiping, stop and shift to something better. Is there something good you want to say about someone? Great, then say that. And even better, wait until they're present and say great things to their face. Use the space below to write about how gossip has made you feel in the past, both giving and receiving it.

....

....

....

....

....

....

....

....

....

....

....

....

....

....

....

....

....

....

....

343. Catch yourself complaining and flip the switch to something better

Kind of like gossip, complaints are low vibe and unhelpful. Try flipping the switch on a complaint to a different kind of statement. Rather than complaining about what you don't like, try a comment about what you do like instead. Use the space below to write that positive version out.

....

....

....

....

....

....

....

....

....

....

....

....

....

....

....

....

....

....

344. Leave a generous tip with a note at a restaurant

If you eat out, write a note on the receipt and leave an extra-generous tip. Notice how this makes you feel. Use the space here to write about the feeling of being generous.

....

....

....

....

....

....

....

....

....

....

....

....

....

....

....

....

....

....

....

....

345. Go to the library and check out a book about happiness

The library might be a place you haven't been to in a while, but it could change everything. Ask for books about happiness, and check one out. Read a chapter. Use the space here to note some of your takeaways from the experience. If you don't want to leave the house, research happiness and read an online article. If you don't want to do that, meditate on the word *happiness* for five minutes and see what comes.

....

....

....

....

....

....

....

....

....

....

....

....

....

....

....

....

....

346. Clean your bathroom

One of the places we spend a lot of time, but also the one we probably avoid cleaning the most. Do an overhaul cleaning session on your bathroom today. Put some elbow grease into it and make it sparkle. Declutter the counter, clean the cabinets and drawers, and organize all your toiletries. Make it easy to find everything and notice how you feel in that cleaner, clearer space. Use the space below to note your thoughts.

....
....
....
....
....
....
....
....
....
....
....
....
....
....
....
....
....

347. Ask yourself, "What turns me on?"

Use the space here to journal about that.

....

....

....

....

....

....

....

....

....

....

....

....

....

....

....

....

....

....

....

....

....

....

....

348. Make a wish on a dandelion

What do you wish for? Use the space below to write it out as if it's already happened. Start with, "I'm so happy and grateful now that. . . "

....

....

....

....

....

....

....

....

....

....

....

....

....

....

....

....

....

....

....

....

349. Go for a walk and collect shells, rocks, or pinecones

What pieces of nature grab your attention? Collect 5-10 nature objects today and then use the space here to write about the one that stands out the most and why.

....

....

....

....

....

....

....

....

....

....

....

....

....

....

....

....

....

....

....

....

....

350. Organize a neighborhood yard sale

Get together with a few neighbors and bond over a joint sale. Choose a date, make signs, and enjoy the event. How does it feel to lead something? Write about everything that brings up in you below.

....
....
....
....
....
....
....
....
....
....
....
....
....
....
....
....
....
....
....
....
....
....
....

351. Dress up and take yourself out to dinner

Whether it's a coffee and croissant, or a full meal, enjoy treating yourself, from getting ready to feeling great about yourself to enjoying the meal. How did it feel to do this for yourself? Have you ever had a meal out alone? Why or why not? Journal about it here.

....

....

....

....

....

....

....

....

....

....

....

....

....

....

....

....

....

....

....

352. Type in "Funny Videos" on YouTube and watch one

If you find one you really love, send the link to someone you know who needs a laugh today. Use the space here to write about how you like incorporating laughter into your moments when you're having a tough day.

....

....

....

....

....

....

....

....

....

....

....

....

....

....

....

....

....

....

....

....

....

353. Type in "Ultimate Dog Tease" on YouTube and watch the video

This is just so funny to me. I hope you enjoy it. What makes you laugh? Write about your sense of humor below.

....

....

....

....

....

....

....

....

....

....

....

....

....

....

....

....

....

....

....

....

354. Buy a singing bowl and practice making it sing

It takes a little practice but once you get the hang of it, making a singing bowl sing is really cool. You can also try doing this on a crystal glass or bowl. How did the sound make you feel? How did accomplishing making the sound make you feel? Use the space below to write about it.

....

....

....

....

....

....

....

....

....

....

....

....

....

....

....

....

....

....

....

....

355. Go a whole day without complaining

Challenge yourself and see what happens. Write about what you noticed here.

....

....

....

....

....

....

....

....

....

....

....

....

....

....

....

....

....

....

....

....

....

....

....

356. Open all your windows

Choose a fair-weather day to go around the house and open every window. Allow the breeze to move the energy and air it all out for at least 15 minutes. As you sit and feel the flow, journal about what you notice.

....

....

....

....

....

....

....

....

....

....

....

....

....

....

....

....

....

....

....

....

357. Write your life manifesto

If you had a manifesto for your life, what would it be? What are you declaring as your intentions, motives, or views? Use the space here to write!

....

....

....

....

....

....

....

....

....

....

....

....

....

....

....

....

....

....

....

....

....

358. What would you do or create if you had every resource you needed?

Spend time writing this out and use the feelings you'd experience as if you've already created this thing or situation. Practice feeling the feelings as you write. What is the essence of that feeling?

....
....
....
....
....
....
....
....
....
....
....
....
....
....
....
....
....
....
....
....

359. Declutter, clean, and clear the health area of your home

According to Feng Shui, the center of your home or room represents health. Think of health in all the ways you can. Today, please research the Bagua Map online and locate the center of your home. What does it look like? How is your health? Take a few moments to declutter, clear, and clean the spaces. Your health affects every single other area of your life. And all the other areas also affect your health. Use the space below to journal about this.

....

....

....

....

....

....

....

....

....

....

....

....

....

....

....

....

....

360. Write about something that makes you excited

Set a timer for five minutes and write without censoring yourself. Write everything that seems important and that comes to you. Notice where the feeling of excitement is in your body. Use the space below.

....

....

....

....

....

....

....

....

....

....

....

....

....

....

....

....

....

....

....

....

....

....

361. Write a power statement

Use the space below to write a powerful statement about yourself. Who are you, and what do you stand for? What matters to you? What helps you feel powerful? Where do you get the feeling of power from?

....

....

....

....

....

....

....

....

....

....

....

....

....

....

....

....

....

....

....

....

....

362. Don't believe everything you think

Remember that your mind thinks based on reactions and habits from past experiences. The you you're creating is different, new, and evolved. You can't get there from your past mindset. Every time you remember to clear your mind of any past limiting belief, you make room for something new, different, healthier, and more aligned. Use the space below to write about what you notice and about what's possible.

....
....
....
....
....
....
....
....
....
....
....
....
....
....
....
....
....
....

363. Learn to rely on your indomitable spirit

Every human has the will to live well. That indomitable spirit is what keeps us hopeful and moving forward. It's always there for us. Rely on that when nothing else is working. You are not just your body and mind. Connect with the spirit within by meditating for five minutes on that higher power and your faith in it. Use the space below to note anything that comes up.

....

....

....

....

....

....

....

....

....

....

....

....

....

....

....

....

....

364. Remember who you are

You are a divine spirit and presence. When things are rough, try to remember who you are, your essence. Shift your perspective to something bigger. Use the space here to write about what that means to you.

....
....
....
....
....
....
....
....
....
....
....
....
....
....
....
....
....
....
....
....
....
....

365. Celebrate being alive with someone you know

It's amazing to be alive. With awareness, we have a choice to infuse our moments with high-vibe energy. It's something to celebrate, for sure. Choose someone you love and celebrate being alive in whatever way feels great. Use the space below and each new day as your blank canvas to create everything you're dreaming of.

....

....

....

....

....

....

....

....

....

....

....

....

....

....

....

....

....

....

IN CONCLUSION

I wrote Good Vibes 365 with a mission to give you a way to shift your energy any moment you choose. With awareness, we have a choice. I choose love, gratitude, joy, compassion, understanding, empathy, and generosity, to name a few high vibes. What are you choosing today? It's up to you.

WITH HUGE APPRECIATION

Thank you to everyone who surrounded me with a similar mission—to do this life in a high-vibe way. You all inspire me so much!

To my book designer, Dino Marino, thanks for infusing the high vibes into every part of this gorgeous book!

To all the teachers on my journey: thank you for leading the way and holding me accountable to this powerful practice.

ABOUT THE AUTHOR

Laura Di Franco, CEO of Brave Healer Productions, specializes in publishing and business strategy for holistic health and wellness professionals. Brave Healer Productions is waking the world up to what's possible with books, programs, courses, writer's groups, and events.

Laura strives to keep herself awake and living fiercely alive, with her first priority being joy, no matter what she's doing. She has a 30-year background in holistic physical therapy and 14 years training in the martial arts, and her company has published over 50 Amazon bestselling books. She's a spoken-word poet, lover of dark chocolate, and has a contagious passion for helping you share brave words build your business. Please visit us at BraveHealer.com

Reach out on social media:

https://www.Facebook.com/BraveHealerbyLaura/

https://www.Instagram.com/BraveHealerProductions

https://www.Twitter.com/Brave_Healer

https://www.linkedin.com/in/laura-di-franco-mpt-1b037a5/

https://www.youtube.com/c/
BraveHealerProductionswithLauraDiFranco

OTHER BOOKS BY LAURA DI FRANCO

Living, Healing, and Tae Kwon Do,
A Memoir to Inspire Your Inner Warrior

Brave Healing, a Guide for Your Journey

How to Have Fun With Your Fear

*The Brave Healer Business Mindset
Transformation Journal*

CO-AUTHORED BOOKS

Your High Vibe Business,
A Workbook for Badass Entrepreneurial Success

Joy Stacking,
A 3-Part Formula for Authentic Success

POETRY BOOKS

Warrior Love,
A Journal to Inspire Your Fiercely Alive Whole Self

Warrior Joy,
A Journal to Inspire Your Fiercely Alive Whole Self

Warrior Soul,
A Journal to Inspire Your Fiercely Alive Whole Self

Warrior Dreams,
A Journal to Inspire Your Fiercely Alive Whole Self

Warrior Desire,
Love Poems to Inspire Your Fiercely Alive Whole Self

JOIN THE BRAVE HEALER WRITER'S CIRCLE

Enjoy writing with a community of authors, experts, and healers. Our writer's circle is for you if you want to become a better writer, stay accountable to your craft, and meet awesome people with similar goals! https://lauradifranco.com/brave-healer-writers-circle/

I write to Feng Shui my soul, and to inspire you to be brave. Remember, you were born, so you're worthy. Your message matters. What if the thing you're a little afraid to share is exactly what someone needs to read to change, or even save, their life? It's time to be brave!

Big love,

Laura

PRODUCTIONS

WORDS THAT CHANGE THE WORLD

THE
BraveHealer
WRITERS Retreat